CARS *of the* 1940s

BY THE AUTO EDITORS OF CONSUMER GUIDE®

Publications International, Ltd.

Louis Weber, CEO
Publications International, Ltd.
7373 North Cicero Avenue
Lincolnwood, Illinois 60712

Permission is never granted for commercial purposes.

ISBN-13: 978-1-4127-7205-1
ISBN-10: 1-4127-7205-2

Manufactured in China.

8 7 6 5 4 3 2 1

Library of Congress Control Number: 2008926156

Credits

Photography:

The editors would like to thank the following people and organizations for supplying the photography that made this book possible. They are listed below, along with the page number(s) of their photos.

Scott Baxter: 59; Ken Beebe: 51, 55, 61; Joe Bohovic: 85; Scott Brandt: 77; Rob Burrington: 53; Chan Bush: 11, 32, 49; Joseph Caro: 60; Chrysler Group Media: 10, 12, 13, 14, 18, 19, 22, 23, 24, 25, 26, 27, 28, 29, 37, 38, 39; Bill Coby: 132; Mirco Decet: 135; Peggy Dyer: 59; Ford Media Archives: 42, 43, 44, 46, 48, 50, 51, 52, 53, 54, 55, 58, 60, 62, 63, 64, 65, 66; Jim Frenak: 114, 117, 118, 119, 120, 121; Diane Garnette: 111; Thomas Glatch: 39, 83, 119, 128, 132, 144, 145, 169, 191, 192; GM Media Archives: 72, 76, 77, 78, 82, 85, 87, 88, 91, 92, 94, 97, 99, 101, 104, 108; Ed Goldberger: 25, 163; David Gooley: 9, 107; Gary Greene: 20, 96; Sam Griffith: 34, 37, 46, 76, 79, 80, 95, 99, 100, 106, 108, 133; Tom Hatcher: 136; Jerry Heasley: 14; John Heilig: 40, 74, 75, 84; Don Heiny: 61, 85; Fergus Hernandes: 151; Jeff Johnson: 86; Bud Juneau: 14, 15, 31, 47, 49, 51, 57, 75, 76, 81, 83, 89, 93, 95, 98, 103, 106, 108, 124, 140, 152, 155, 168, 184; Milton Kieft: 18, 27, 32, 35, 44, 58, 86, 90, 105, 109, 139, 160; Nick Komic: 122; Richard Langworth: 126; Rick Lenz: 130; Dan Lyons: 54, 100, 104, 156, 157, 170, 171, 178, 179; Vince Manocchi: 12, 14, 15, 17, 18, 19, 21, 33, 35, 41, 45, 46, 50, 52, 53, 56, 57, 58, 62, 73, 74, 75, 76, 79, 80, 81, 82, 83, 87, 90, 94, 100, 101, 103, 104, 105, 107, 111, 114, 115, 116, 125, 132, 142, 146, 153, 154, 156, 158, 160, 161, 162, 163, 176, 177, 178, 179, 180; Doug Mitchel: 11, 12, 15, 16, 17, 29, 30, 31, 33, 66, 67, 74, 78, 80, 87, 88, 93, 94, 97, 100, 101, 102, 111, 123, 130, 133, 137, 152, 161, 163, 167, 169, 188, 189; M. H. Montgomery: 149; Mike Moore: 130; Mike Mueller: 67, 99, 165, 191, 192; David Newhardt: 35; Clay Nichols: 47; Robert Nicholson: 46, 73; Morton Oppenheimer: 109; Nina Padgett: 23, 24, 81, 86, 91; Jay Peck: 41, 83, 93; Chris Ranck: 172; Jeff Rose: 36; Tom Shaw: 123; Gary Smith: 19, 20, 48, 108, 139, 141, 147, 153, 155; Richard Spiegelman: 26, 190; Steve Statham: 174; Cassie Stone: 84, 89; Tom Storm: 110; David Temple: 56, 150, 151, 154; Jim Thompson: 185; Phil Toy: 15, 82; H. J. Wagner, Jr.: 27; W. C. Waymack: 28, 30, 33, 37, 39, 40, 54, 57, 60, 65, 67, 73, 78, 79, 84, 95, 96, 102, 104, 108, 113, 122, 124, 129, 133, 138, 146, 156, 164, 170; Joseph Wherry: 8, 9, 141; Hub Wilson: 131; Nicky Wright: 18, 27, 31, 36, 43, 46, 56, 64, 75, 98, 109, 129, 147, 158; Zoom Photo: 38, 65

Front Cover: Ron Kimball/www.kimballstock.com
Back Cover: Bud Juneau; Vince Manocchi; Doug Mitchel; Richard Spiegelman; W. C. Waymack
Title Page: W. C. Waymack

Owners:

Special thanks to the owners of the cars featured in this book for their cooperation. Their names and the page numbers for their vehicles follow.

AACA Museum: 40; Joe Abela: 26; Al Adams: 31, back cover; George Adams: 38; David Aikew: 85; Erik Akins 89; William Albright: 114, 115; Nick Alexander: 53, 62; Jean Allan: 40; Farnum Alston: 14; Jim Anderson: 73; John Andreason: 89; Gordon Apker: 96; Don Armacost, Jr.: 172; Jim and Mary Ashworth: 95; Art Astor: 21, 33, 82; Melvin Atkin: 31; Dale Aylward: 189; David Baird 164; George Ball: 60; Thomas Barratt III: 158; Ed Barwick: 168; Nelson Bates: 151; Alan Baumer: 78; William Baumgartner: 65; Buzz and Fran Beckman: 169; Chuck Beed: 163; Blackhawk Collection: 15; John Blackowski: 83; Gary Bohannon: 83; Norman and Joyce Booth: 50; Larry and Beverly Bowman: 33; Robert Bradley: 32; Carroll and Dawn Bramble: 30; Edward Bratton: 171; Elmer Brawn: 94; Edward Brehm: 137; Robert Brelsford: 14, 19; Bob Briggs: 76; Ron Brooks: 80; Ed and Edna Brown: 123; Richard Brune: 146; Jack Buchannan: 64; Donald and Phyllis Bueter: 165; James Buffington: 15; Nicola Bulgari: 74, 75, 84; Mike Callahan: 102; Dave Cammack: 185; Lawrence Camuso: 82; Robert Carlson: 27; Benjamin Caskey: 65; Penny Casteele: 114; Jim Chernock: 110; Chevs 'N Vettes of Scottsdale: 109; Ed Cholakian: 109; Jere Clark: 75; Edward and Arlene Cobb: 170; Dr. Steven Colsen: 99; Herman Cox: 59; Lloyd Crabtree: 79; Tom Crooks: 73; Donald Curtis: 160; Raymond Dade: 176, 177; Vincent Daul: 25; Herb Rothman and Ted Davidson: 163; Terry Davies: 141, title page; W. E. Davis: 124; Al DeFabrizio: 192; Ellis DeGrange: 46; Harry DeMenge: 18, 35, back cover; Donald Desing: 16; Richard DeVecchi: 81; Tony Donna: 57; Ken Dunsir: 111; Richard Wayne Durham: 57; Bud Dutton: 101; Lloyd Duzell: 46; Jim Dworschack: 144; Glen Eisenhamer: 87; Vern Ellis: 119; Wilbert Endres: 170; Harold Evans: 95; Paul Fadgen: 178; Fairway Chevrolet: 81, 86, 91; Bev Ferreira: 184; Angelo Finaldi: 101; Fraser Dante Ltd.: 93, 125; Terri Gardner: 163; Jerry Garvin: 162; Stan Gautz: 139; Ralph Geissler: 155; Joe Gergits: 108; Roger Gibb: 156; Sonny and Maci Glasbrenner: 165; Ken Gominsky, Sr.: 74; Jim Grace: 104; Clifford Greenwalt: 67, back cover; Lee Greer: 83; Ken Griesemer: 132; Ed Gunther: 31, 106; Bernie Hackett: 83; Bill Halliday: 107; Rosemarie Hansen: 145; Von Hardesty: 136; John Hare: 111; William Harper: 66; Ben and Jean Harwood: 155; Ronald Hasemann: 73; Ron Haulman: 108; Ken Havekost: 141, 143, 147; Harvey Hedgecock: 130; John Heinaman: 58; Ross Helco: 114; Edward Hess: 111; Tom Hincz: 111; Harold Hoeferlin: 39; Eldon and Esta Hoestetler: 113; Phillip and Nancy Hoffman: 47; David Holb: 48; James Hollingsworth: 150, 154; Dave Holls: 153; David Holmes: 56; Ken Holste: 169; Bill Hubert: 129, 132, 133; A. W. Huffman, Jr.: 51, 55, 61; James and Marian Humlong: 19, 20; Ken Huusfeldt: 153; Victor Jacobellis: 133; Chris and Pete Jakubowski: 102; Roger James: 86; Jeremy Janss: 163; Robert Jarrett: 43; Joe and Chris Jelinski: 59; Blaine Jenkins: 27, 98; Lewis Jenkins: 84; Bob Johnson: 41; Ralph Johnson: 92; Dick Johnston: 58; Joseph Leir Memorial Auto Collection: 21, 33; Bud Juneau: 103; Press and Janet Kale: 125; Mike Kaminsky: 79; Gene Kappel: 156; Jack Karleskind: 49; Roger Kash: 97; John Kepich: 156; Lawrence Kessler: 95; Larry Klein: 98; Ron Korb: 108; Robert and Sandi Kostka: 158; Richard Krist: 45; Richard Kughn: 56; Ron and Debbie Ladley: 187; Ronald Laird: 102; Roger Lamm: 161; Larry Lange: 78; Wesley Lantz: 9; Chris Lapp: 86; Robert Wagner and Robert Lasher: 35; William Lauer: 116, 162; Jerry and Adell Laurin: 128; James Lauzon: 157; Jim Laverdiere: 32; Bob and Phyllis Leach: 8, 9; Thomas Lerch: 44; Dr. Gerald Levitt: 85; Fred Lewis: 88; Russel Liechty: 36; Gary Loomer: 41; Robert Loudon: 138; Les Ludwig: 9; Eugene Luning: 156; Larry and Jan Malone: 96; David Marshall: 190, back cover; Larry Martin: 37, 104; Lloyd and Martha Mayes: 23, 24; Al Maynard: 188; Robert McAtee: 15, 161; William Lauer and Robert McAtee: 17; Dave McConnell: 104; Garry McGee: 102; Dick McKean: 100; Allen McWade: 61; Tom Meleo: 76, 100; Ray Menefee: 75; Robert Messinger: 90; Alan Mest: 60; Paul and Mary Meyer: 84; David Miller: 153; Jack Miller: 118, 119, 120, 121; Jim Miller: 76; Rod Miller: 73; S. Ray Miller, Jr.: 43, 61; Jack Minton: 104; Robert Montgomery: 79; Jim Moran: 74; Tom Morgan: 30; Rod Morris: 99; Joe Moss: 16; Verl Mowery: 37; Jim Mueller: 123; National Automobile Museum: 15, 129; Tenny Natkin: 106; Ralph Neubauer: 12; Charles Newton: 148; Clay Nichols: 47; Emily Tax and Roger Nichols: 174; Harry Nicks: 94; Oceanside Police Officers' Association: 18; John Oliver III: 35, 36; Roland Olm: 191, 192; Michael Olson: 144; Monty Ostberg: 11; John Otto: 122; Robert Paige: 14; Donald Passardi: 54; Ruben Polanco: 180; John Poochigian: 81; Michael Porto: 146; Anthony Pounds-Cornish: 135; Ken Poynter: 117; Dan Prager: 45; Joel Prescott: 90; Dick Pyle: 37, 80; B. C. Pyle: 191; Gerald Quam: 101; Rader's Relics: 67; Terry Radey: 75; Ramshead Collection: 57; Vito Ranks: 17; Tricia Redolme: 142; Robert Reeves: 50; Charles Regnerus: 121; Henry and Joan Rehm: 46; Myron Reichert: 105; David Reidy: 151; Bill Reinhardt: 132; Glen and Vera Reints: 167; Raymond Reis, Sr.: 20; Tom Rohrich: 105; Ed Rouhe: 49; Robert Russell: 152; Charles Ruvolo: 122; Arthur Sabin: 130, 133; Harold Sage: 87; Hannes Schachtner: 80; Jerry Schlorff: 18; William and Joseph Schoenbeck: 100; William Schwanbeck: 79; Larry and Judy Scott: 53; Jon Segedy: 125; Nelson and Evelyn Sembach: 58; Jim and Mary Shanahan: 12; John Shanahan: 154; Donald Sharp: 109; Leonard Shaw: 93, back cover; Raymond Silva, Jr.: 107; Dave and June Simon: 87; John Slusar: 39; Henry Smith: 32; H. Robert and Kathryn Stamp: 191; Carmi Standish: 151; Danny Steine: 41; Richard Stevenson: 45; Suburban Motors: 25; Edward Swoboda: 54; Eugene Tareshawty: 152; Erica Tenney: 179; Eugene and Catherine Thomas: 180; Mick Thrasher: 77; Neil Torrence: 160; Chuck and Mark VanDerVelde: 93; Burt VanFlue: 178, 179; Thomas Venezia: 43; George and Celine Voris: 74; Bill and Lila Walker: 140; Bob Ward: 67; Dr. Irv Warren: 50; Anthony and Eloise Wells: 109; Bobby Wiggins: 76, 95, 100; Roy Wiggins, Jr.: 56; Phil Wilder: 46; Al Wilkiewicz: 52; John Williams: 98, 103; Woody World: 192; Harry Wynn: 51; Tony Yenne: 28; Marvin Yount, Jr.: 139; Joseph and Glenna Zaborny: 33

Special thanks to the photographic and media services groups of the following organizations: Chrysler LLC; Ford Motor Company: General Motors Corporation

CONTENTS

FOREWORD

World War II tested America's "greatest genera-
tion" in ways the Great Depression had not.
While countless thousands fought and died for
freedom in far-away places, millions on the home
front endured hardships in daily life and hard
work producing stupendous quantities of military
goods. It was a time of national unity unlike any
before—or since.

America's automakers did their part to hasten
victory, and most returned to peacetime with
money to spend and boundless optimism. So did
most Americans. One result was a fevered postwar seller's market born of a soaring new national prosperity. With that, the American automobile,
like the country itself, was never the same.

As artifacts of a momentous era in U.S. history, the cars of the 1940s remain a compelling
fascination, just as the war continues to resonate
in American society and politics. We hope this
book will help you to appreciate both.

Small cars were never big business in pre-World War II America, but it wasn't for lack of proponents. Among the most energetic was Roy S. Evans, who took over the American Austin Car Company in 1935 with hopes of succeeding where Sir Herbert Austin had failed.

The British auto magnate had set up a plant in Butler, Pennsylvania, to build his Austin Seven, a 1920s-era "light car" of the type popular abroad. Butler had ready access to raw materials, workers, and East Coast ports, all of which allowed budget pricing of well under $500. And production of the gas-sipping midget began in early 1930, just as the Depression was setting in. But though the timing was right, the public was wary of the slow, spindly Seven, and American Austin went bankrupt after building fewer than 20,000 cars.

Evans got the place for just $5000, then fast paid off debts, secured a fat $250,000 government loan, and hired top-name talent to update the aging Austin design. The result appeared in 1936 as the American Bantam with a heavier frame, assorted mechanical improvements, and contemporary Detroit-like styling. The makeover cost a mere $7000, so pricing was little changed. But despite the addition of winsome new models, sales were never strong, and dwindled quickly after 1937. Bantam struggled into 1941, then ended car production at fewer than 5000 total—worse than American Austin's performance.

Meantime, Bantam's small-car expertise helped land a contract to design what became the World War II Jeep. Bantam built the first prototype, and hoped for a huge windfall as sole supplier of the four-wheel-drive "general purpose" vehicle. But the Army thought Bantam was too small to build all the Jeeps required, so it brought in Ford and Willys, resulting in a three-way design and manufacturing effort. But where the two big companies built more than 600,000 wartime Jeeps, Bantam's order was a mere 2943. However, a second contract led Bantam to manufacture utility trailers during and after the war. The company ceased operations in 1956.

1

2

3

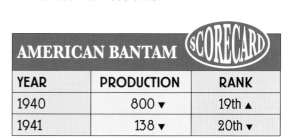

4

1. The priciest 1940 American Bantam was the $565 woodie wagon. 2. All 1940 American Bantams were powered by a 50-cid four-cylinder engine that put out 22 horsepower. The Custom Club roadster had dummy louvers on the front fenders. 3-4. Speedsters had cut-down doors and marginal four-passenger capacity. Their sweeping bodyside coves invited two-tone paint treatments. 5. The new-for-1940 Hollywood convertible boasted a cabriolet-style top and leather seats. 6. At 1211 pounds, the Master roadster was the lightest 1941 model. Total American Bantam production in 1940-41 was less than 1000 units.

5

6

AMERICAN BANTAM	SCORECARD	
YEAR	PRODUCTION	RANK
1940	800 ▼	19th ▲
1941	138 ▼	20th ▼

In 1924, Walter P. Chrysler, a former head of General Motors' Buick division, took over ailing Maxwell-Chalmers to launch a car—and a company—all his own. That first Chrysler boasted engineering advances like four-wheel hydraulic brakes and high-compression engines, plus attractive styling and competitive prices. It couldn't miss, and it didn't. By 1929, it had earned WPC more than enough money to acquire the Dodge Brothers Company and to introduce the DeSoto and Plymouth brands, thus creating a GM-like rival to the industry leader itself.

The Depression slowed Chrysler Corporation's meteoric rise, as did a costly gamble on the innovative but unpopular 1934 Chrysler and DeSoto Airflow "streamliners." Yet these setbacks were far from devastating, and recovery was both quick and strong. Indeed, Chrysler overtook Ford Motor Company as the nation's second-largest automaker in 1936, and would hold that rank until 1952.

Walter P. Chrysler died in 1940, but his chosen successor as president, K. T. Keller, continued his successful policies of conservative, practical styling and dull but sturdy straight-six and straight-eight engines. Cleverly, all models in this decade, from low-priced Plymouth to opulent Chrysler Imperial, shared a basic chassis and bodyshells that were changed only twice (for 1940-41 and again for '49). Boring perhaps, but there were flashes of glamour, such as the wood-bodied 1941-42 Chrysler Town & Country station wagons and the equally striking convertibles and sedans that followed postwar. Other notables include the versatile 1946-49 DeSoto Suburban and Carry-All sedans with fold-down rear seats; a bevy of limousine-like long-wheelbase sedans; the winsome 1949 Dodge Wayfarer two-seat roadster; and the 1949 Plymouth DeLuxe Suburban, a pioneering all-steel station wagon.

Chrysler compiled a distinguished production record during World War II and was financially robust when peace returned. Alas, Keller's insistence on boxy styling proved an increasing liability against GM and Ford once the postwar seller's market ended in 1950 and cutthroat competition resumed. Thus began the series of boom-and-bust business cycles that have plagued Chrysler ever since.

1

2

3

4

1. Chrysler Corporation founder Walter P. Chrysler stands with a 1940 version of his namesake. It would be the last new Chrysler he would live to introduce. **2.** Arriving as a Chrysler exclusive for 1939, Fluid Drive was essentially a conventional three-speed manual transmission that had both a clutch and a fluid coupling between the engine and transmission, which allowed stopping in any gear and starting off again without using the clutch. **3.** Six Chrysler models on wheelbases of 122.5 to 145.5 inches spanned a price range of $895 to $2445. Lower-line offerings used a 241.5-cubic-inch six of 108-112 horsepower; upper models a 323.5-cid straight eight of 132-143 hp. Anchoring the line was the Royal, shown here as a $960 coupe. **4.** DeSoto occupied the second rung of the Chrysler Corporation ladder. Most models rode a 122.5-inch wheelbase and all had a 228.1-cid six of 100-105 hp. Topping the standard-length DeSoto line for 1940 was the dapper $1095 Custom convertible.

1

2

3

1. All-new sheetmetal on a longer 119.5-inch wheelbase differentiated the 1940 **Dodges** from their 1939 counterparts. Situated one step below DeSotos in size, price, and power, Dodges came with an 87-horsepower 218-cubic-inch inline six in Special or DeLuxe guise. Shown is an $815 Special two-door sedan. **2.** By far the most popular Dodge was the $905 DeLuxe four-door sedan. **3.** After a one-year hiatus, a convertible returned to the Dodge line in the form of a $1030 Deluxe model. As such, it cost $65 less than its DeSoto Custom counterpart.

1. As it had been since its introduction in 1928, Plymouth remained Chrysler Corporation's entry-level car, competing directly against Chevrolet and Ford. Standard models sat on a 117.5-inch wheelbase, and all carried a 201-cubic-inch six-cylinder engine rated at 84-87 horsepower, though a low-compression 65-hp "economy" version was also available. Roadking and DeLuxe trim levels were offered, with prices starting at $645 for this Roadking business coupe. **2.** Unique in the low-price field were Plymouth's extended-length seven-passenger sedan and limousine on a 137-inch wheelbase. The sedan sold for $1005, the limo for $1080, but neither was very popular. **3.** Plymouth offered woodie wagons in both trim levels; the more expensive DeLuxe version (shown) started at $970. **4.** One of New York's finest scrutinizes a fresh batch of 1940 Plymouths.

1940		SCORECARD
MAKE	**PRODUCTION**	**RANK**
CHRYSLER	92,419 ▲	10th ▲
DeSOTO	65,467 ▲	13th ●
DODGE	195,505 ▲	6th ▼
PLYMOUTH	423,155 ▲	3rd ●

1

2

3

1. **Chrysler's** least-expensive ragtop for 1941 was the six-cylinder Windsor at $1315. 2. The first of the famous Town & Country wagons appeared for 1941. Bodywork aft of the cowl was made of mahogany-veneered panels outlined with white ash framing. Six- and nine-passenger versions were offered only in the Windsor series starting at $1412. 3. Both the six-cylinder Windsor convertible and the eight-cylinder New Yorker convertible offered optional Highlander plaid upholstery. 4. The least-expensive eight-cylinder Chrysler was the $1245 Saratoga business coupe. It had only a front bench seat, but the trunk was huge.

4

1

2

3

1. Chrysler sedans, including the $1165 Windsor, were fitted with rear-hinged back doors, sometimes referred to as "suicide doors." **2.** Chrysler sent this streamlined dual-cowl phaeton on the show-car circuit during 1941. Called the Newport, it previewed a name that would later be applied to the company's 1950 hardtops. **3.** New for 1941 and offered in all Chrysler series was the town sedan body style, which combined conventional front-hinged rear doors with blanked-out rear roof pillars. Shown is the top-line $1760 Crown Imperial version, which rode the New Yorker's wheelbase rather than the longer span applied to other Crown Imperials. **4.** Another of Chrysler's '40s show cars was the Thunderbolt, a humongous two-seat convertible with a retractable hardtop that back flipped into the trunk. It sported the hidden headlights that would soon show up on DeSotos.

4

1

2

1. A facelift for '41 brought a vertical-bar grille that would remain a DeSoto trademark well into the Fifties. It also spurred the brand's popularity, moving the company from 13th to 10th in industry sales. DeSoto remained a step ahead of Dodge on the Chrysler Corporation ladder, with a slightly bigger engine (though still only a six), slightly larger dimensions, and slightly higher prices. A classy Custom convertible cost $1240. This example wears period accessories including fog lamps, spotlights, and bumper overrider bars. **2.** The "long hood, long deck" look of a Custom business coupe could be yours for $982.

A FLUID DRIVING SUMMER thanks to Dodge

SMOOTHEST CARS AFLOAT—

IT'S ship, ship AHOY— and anchors aweigh, as you too become the happy master and skipper of a Dodge Propeller-Driven Cruiser. Here are the smoothest things afloat on any highway. The sleekest in any traffic. The lowest priced and the fastest-selling cars with Fluid Drive in all the world. This means that your own good buying judgment has already been confirmed a hundred thousand times and more— by other brand-new Captains of these Dodge Fluid Drive Cruisers. ¶ They'll tell you it's a new day in motorcars, and you might better be in on it while these Dodge prices last and drive forevermore without constant clutching and shifting as of old. Your foot now does tirelessly almost all the things your arms and body used to do in ordinary cars. The daintiest slipper, too, will command these power-giants, and they'll behave for "her" like handsome, well-trained servants. TUNE IN MAJOR BOWES, C.B.S., THURSDAYS, 9 TO 10 P.M., E.D.S.T.

SAFETY-RIM WHEELS GUARD YOUR TIRES AND YOU

FULL-FLOATING RIDE FOR A "RIDING ZONE" WITH COMPLETE SHOCK PROTECTION

FLOATING POWER ENGINE MOUNTINGS CRADLE YOUR ENGINE FOR LONG LIFE

SAFETY-STEEL BODY FOR MAXIMUM SAFETY AND YOUR PEACE OF MIND

MASTER HYDRAULIC BRAKES FOR EQUAL-PRESSURE BRAKING EFFICIENCY AND SAFETY

DODGE FLUID DRIVE DRIVING BECOMES GLIDING AS YOU RULE THE ROAD

FINGER-TIP STEERING FOR SWEETER, SMOOTHER HANDLING AT THE WHEEL

ALL-FLUID DRIVE *Dodge* FLUID DRIVE $25 EXTRA Car Prices Subject to Change Without Notice

1

2

3

1. Dodge promoted its newly available Fluid Drive semi-automatic transmission using colorful language with a nautical note. While its $25 option price sounds like a bargain, it represents about 2.5 percent of the cost of a 1941 Dodge, equal to roughly $500 today. **2.** A 1941 facelift brought Dodges a "bird wing" grille and small tailfin-like taillights. Series designations changed from Special and DeLuxe to DeLuxe and Custom. A Custom club coupe sold for $995. **3.** Priced $63 above its traditional sedan counterpart was the new-for-'41 town sedan with blanked-out rear quarter windows. It was offered only in top-line Custom trim for $1082.

1

2

1. A mild facelift updated Plymouths for 1941 as did a change in model designations. Roadking was retired, leaving DeLuxe as the entry-level series with Special DeLuxe becoming the new line-topper. A snappy Special DeLuxe business coupe went for $795. **2.** Blackout models, which lacked chrome trim, were built for military use. **3.** At the opposite end of the spectrum was this cheery $1007 Special DeLuxe convertible. **4.** A Special DeLuxe woodie wagon sold for $1031. **5.** Though they were hardly impressive performers, many Plymouths found their way into police duty.

3

4

5

1941		SCORECARD
MAKE	PRODUCTION	RANK
CHRYSLER	161,704 ▲	8th ▲
DeSOTO	97,497 ▲	10th ▲
DODGE	237,002 ▲	7th ▼
PLYMOUTH	545,811 ▲	3rd ●

2

1

1. Horizontal grille bars that wrapped around into the front fenders distinguished the 1942 Chryslers. The six-cylinder engine in Royals and Windsors grew from 241 to 250 cubic inches, bringing 120 horsepower. Saratogas, New Yorkers, and Crown Imperials kept their 140-hp 323-cubic-inch eight. The New Yorker sedan was priced at $1475. **2.** A Chrysler promotional shot included sketches depicting "the cars of tomorrow." **3-4.** The Windsor line hosted the Town & Country woodie wagon, which started at $1595. Due to the onset of World War II, Chryslers built after January 1, 1942, had body-color rather than chrome trim; these cars were known as "blackout specials." Civilian production ceased on the 29th of that month.

3

4

1

1-3. The 1942 DeSoto was famous for sporting the first hidden headlights since the '37 Cord. Meanwhile, a wraparound trim strip was added above the grille, and massive bumpers replaced the thinner ones used previously. Shown is a $1142 Custom club coupe. **4.** Convertibles were offered in both the DeLuxe and Custom series for 1942. This $1317 Custom convertible wears white wheel trim rings intended to simulate whitewall tires. The six-cylinder DeSoto engine grew from 228 to 236 cubic inches, pushing horsepower from 105 to 115. With the start of World War II, DeSotos built after January 1, 1942, were "blackout specials," and civilian production ceased on February 9.

2

3

4

1. Stouter bumpers and a heavy chrome grille graced 1942 Dodges, along with fenders that flowed more smoothly into the bodysides. Engines increased from 217.8 cubic inches to 230.2, boosting horsepower from 91 to 105. DeLuxe and Custom series returned, but the convertible was again offered only in Custom guise at $1245. 2. The jaunty club coupe bodystyle was extended to the DeLuxe line for 1942, but the example shown is the $1045 Custom, which cost $50 more than its DeLuxe counterpart. 3. Dodge's most popular car by far was the $1048 four-door sedan with its rear-hinged "suicide" back doors. Due to the war effort, cars built after January 1, 1942, were "blackout specials," with chrome bumpers but painted trim, and civilian production ceased for the duration in early February.

7 BEAUTIFUL VERSIONS OF ONE GREAT STORY!

FOUR-DOOR SEDAN—Notice the extra length and low-to-the-road design of this handsome new Plymouth sedan. Two-color interiors are tailored in fabrics that harmonize with body colors.

CONVERTIBLE COUPE—This smart Plymouth is your ideal all-weather car. It has the famous power-operated top...goes up or down at a touch. Seat cushions are upholstered in red leather.

CLUB COUPE—Here's six-passenger seating capacity with extraordinary roominess. There's a huge luggage compartment in the rear...outside door locks on both sides for your convenience.

STATION WAGON—A grand car for town or country...with natural finish or 2-tone body. Both rear seats are removable and interchangeable, providing great flexibility.

They're Brilliant Automobiles —Plymouth's Finest! Choose any model and you get great new power...new economy...a smooth, new ride. Plymouth's your wise low-priced car buy!

Look them over—the finest cars Plymouth ever built—big, roomy, low-slung beauties, with great new power and new economy. Plymouth's Finest is your wise investment in driving satisfaction.

You get a massive, new-styled front end ...concealed running boards...lovely new interiors in colors that harmonize with the body. The low-to-the-road design adds to stability and safety, and you enjoy a wonderfully smooth, gentle ride.

Plymouth's Finest has a big 95-horsepower engine—most powerful of "All Three" low-priced cars—yet you actually enjoy new economy as well! The big engine breezes along with fewer revolutions per mile...saving gasoline and oil...lengthening engine life. In all normal driving, you use only a fraction of Plymouth's tremendous power.

Plymouth has always been famous for advanced engineering and precision manufacturing. In this Plymouth you get such long-life features as an Oil Bath Air Cleaner, Oil Filter, Coil Springs, patented Floating Power engine mountings, Superfinished engine parts...advantages that help make Plymouth "the car that stands up best."

All over the world, motorists know "Plymouth Builds Great Cars." And this is the finest car in Plymouth history...finest in performance, finest in materials, finest in workmanship. Any way you judge, it's your wise low-priced car buy.

See this great car at your nearby Plymouth dealer's—ride in it—and, by all means, *drive* it! All prices and specifications are subject to change without notice. Plymouth Division of Chrysler Corporation.

HEAR MAJOR BOWES, THURSDAYS, C. B. S. NETWORK

PRODUCTS OF CHRYSLER CORPORATION

Army Tanks • Anti-Aircraft Guns • Aircraft Parts
Army Vehicles • Passenger Cars • Trucks • Marine
& Industrial Engines • Diesel Engines • Oilite Bearings • Airtemp Heating and Air Conditioning.

TOWN SEDAN—Here's a smart new design to win admiration wherever you go—a low, rakish car—styled to stay beautiful for years to come! All Plymouths have rotary-type safety door latches.

COUPE—For business or pleasure, this smart Plymouth Coupe is a wise investment. It has tremendous luggage space. All Plymouth models have wide, concealed running boards.

TWO-DOOR SEDAN—Here's the ideal car for families with young children; they are safely beyond reach of any doors when in the rear seat. *Interior light goes on when right front door is opened.

*On Special De Luxe models.

Buy Wisely_BUY PLYMOUTH

CHRYSLER CORPORATION'S NO. 1 CAR _THE QUALITY CAR WITH ECONOMY

1

2

3

1. "Plymouth's Finest" arrived for 1942 with a redesign that brought lower, wider bodies and a broad grille. Engine size and power also increased, from 201.3 cubic inches and 87-92 horsepower to 217.8 cid and 95 hp—enough that Plymouth could boast that it was the "most powerful of 'All Three' low-priced cars" (meaning Plymouth, Chevrolet, and Ford). 2. A Special DeLuxe convertible cost $1078. Most noticeable on light-colored cars was the new sheetmetal "apron" that appeared below the front bumper. 3. Per government mandate, "blackout" cars were built in the final days of prewar assembly, with virtually all exterior trim save the bumpers being painted rather than chromed.

1942	SCORECARD	
MAKE	**PRODUCTION**	**RANK**
CHRYSLER	36,586 ▼	10th ▼
DeSOTO	24,015 ▼	13th ▼
DODGE	68,522 ▼	6th ▲
PLYMOUTH	152,427 ▼	3rd ●

1946

1. As was the case with most brands, Chrysler's early post-war cars were simply warmed-over 1942 models—with greatly increased prices. But one change in the lineup was a variation in the Town & Country offerings. Gone were the traditional six- and nine-passenger wagons; in their place was a sedan and convertible, both with signature wood trim. Prototype hardtop coupes and a two-door brougham (replica shown) were also built, but not sold to the public. 2. A convertible Town & Country bodyshell is fitted with its wood paneling. 3. Comedian Bob Hope stands with a Town & Country convertible. At $2743, it was Chrysler's most expensive regular-length model.

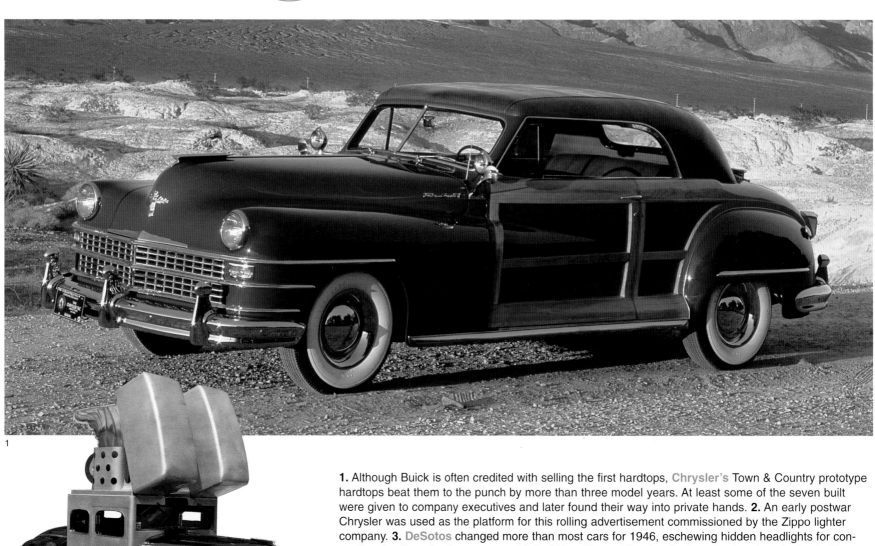

1. Although Buick is often credited with selling the first hardtops, **Chrysler's** Town & Country prototype hardtops beat them to the punch by more than three model years. At least some of the seven built were given to company executives and later found their way into private hands. **2.** An early postwar Chrysler was used as the platform for this rolling advertisement commissioned by the Zippo lighter company. **3. DeSotos** changed more than most cars for 1946, eschewing hidden headlights for conventional units, adopting a crowned full-width grille, and flowing the front fenders into the bodysides. Shown is the new-for-'46 Suburban, which was built on the long-wheelbase chassis of the seven-passenger sedan, but it seated eight and came with two-tone paint and a roof rack. **4.** A top-line Custom convertible tipped the price scale at $1761, a stout $444 heavier than a comparable '42. **5.** A similar car in the **Dodge** lineup was the $1649 Custom convertible. A new face greeted postwar buyers, and—as on the DeSoto—the front fenders stretched into the doors.

3

4

5

1

2

1. If you liked the 1942 Plymouth, you'd probably like the '46 as well; the grille changed slightly, but little else was new. Cars were in such short supply after the war that it took a stroke of luck in addition to the $1199 list price to buy this Special DeLuxe two-door sedan. **2.** Plymouth ads of the day touted value, but they were hardly necessary; nearly all automakers sold all the cars they could build—often before they could even build them. **3.** Plymouth's wood-sided wagon remained the costliest model in the lineup, though now it was costlier still. The base price jumped by 35 percent to $1539.

3

1946 SCORECARD		
MAKE	PRODUCTION	RANK
CHRYSLER	83,310 ▲	11th ▼
DeSOTO	66,900 ▲	12th ▲
DODGE	163,490 ▲	4th ▲
PLYMOUTH	264,660 ▲	3rd ●
All figures estimated		

1

2

1. **Chrysler's** wood-sided Town & Country convertible came only in eight-cylinder form on a 127.5-inch wheelbase. Base price rose again, to just shy of $3000. 2. The other Town & Country offering was a four-door sedan, which came with a six-cylinder engine on a 121.5-inch wheelbase for $2713. 3. An eight-cylinder Saratoga four-door sedan listed for $1973. 4. A New Yorker fitted with a white padded top was offered by J.T. Fisher Motor Co., a dealership in Memphis. 5. The "long hood, short deck" look that would become popular decades later was previewed—in gigantic scale—on New Yorker club coupes. This example has been customized by coachbuilder Derham with a padded white top and wicker windowsill trim.

3

4

5

1

2

3

4

1-3. A **DeSoto** Custom club coupe cost $1591, but that was before adding the optional two-tone paint, right-side mirror, and whitewall tires. Like all Chrysler Corporation cars of this period, it carried a third brake light above the license plate. **4.** If you needed to seat eight passengers, the $2283 Custom Suburban was a great way to do it. Suburbans rode a 139.5-inch wheelbase, 18 inches longer than that of the standard models.

1

1. After its first postwar models were introduced with a surprisingly elaborate facelift, Dodge carried them over into 1947 virtually unchanged—except for price. This Custom convertible went up $222 to $1871. 2. A Custom four-door sedan also cost more for '47; up $118 to $1507. 3. A Custom interior shows off its woodgrain dash paint and simple (by today's standards) door trim. 4. The least-expensive Dodge was the DeLuxe three-passenger business coupe at $1347. 5. Four-door sedans retained their "suicide" rear-hinged back doors; only the pricier town sedan had traditional rear doors.

2

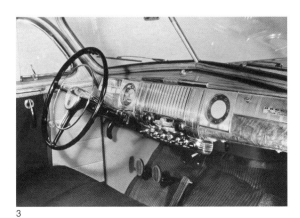

3

4

5

1

"Here they come, Mom! And Jim won't need the wish-bone—they've got their PLYMOUTH!"

4

2

3

5

1. Plymouths had been freshened after the war and entered 1947 with little more than a price increase. Unlike others in the Chrysler Corporation fleet, Plymouths retained their boxy front fenders and didn't offer Fluid Drive. A Special DeLuxe business coupe sold for $1209. **2.** A Special DeLuxe four-door sedan, Plymouth's traditional top seller, listed for $1289. **3-4.** Early postwar buyers often had to put their name on a list and wait for a car to come in. Jim's evidently arrived just in time for Christmas dinner. **5.** While any new car was a source of pride, a $1565 Special DeLuxe convertible was a cause for envy.

1947		*s*CORECARD
MAKE	**PRODUCTION**	**RANK**
CHRYSLER	119,260 ▲	9th ▲
DeSOTO	87,000 ▲	12th ●
DODGE	243,160 ▲	5th ▼
PLYMOUTH	382,290 ▲	3rd ●
All figures estimated		

1. **Chryslers** went virtually unchanged again for 1948—except for the usual price hikes—and would carry on as "first series" '49s. A New Yorker club coupe shot up more than $300 to $2385. **2.** Two-toned both inside and out, the $2163 Windsor Traveler came standard with a wood roof rack. **3.** Although oddly proportioned, a $2285 New Yorker business coupe boasted eight-cylinder power and enough trunk space to move a small kingdom.

1

2

3

1. DeSotos were essentially unchanged for 1948, and carried into the following year as "first series" '49s. Due to their expansive room, long-wheelbase Suburbans were sometimes used as taxis. **2.** A Custom club coupe went for $1874 before adding this car's optional fog lights, grille guard, and sun visor. **3.** A Custom convertible topped $2000 for the first time, reaching $2296. **4. Dodges** were also virtual carryovers and also extended into 1949's "first series." The Custom convertible cost $2198 and came with a solid-color dash instead of the woodgrain-painted dash found in other models. **5.** A Custom club coupe cost $1774. This body style was not offered in the lower-line DeLuxe series. **6.** The popular Custom four-door sedan rose $281 to $1788. **7.** The stretched seven-passenger version cost $2179.

4

5

6

7

Why do you see so many
PLYMOUTH taxicabs?

The answer makes it a great car for YOU, too!

Taxicab operators *have* to know automobiles. They select cars that can take it—in all kinds of weather, on all kinds of streets—often on a 24-hour-a-day schedule. They insist that their taxicabs be safe, smooth-riding, easy to handle, economical to maintain and—above all—*dependable*.

That's why taxicab operators—throughout the country—today use far more *Plymouths* than any other make of car. In fact, *Plymouth* is the best car for you, too!

Look what you get with Plymouth—as standard equipment, at no extra cost. You get bigger, faster

Super-Cushion Tires on new, wider *Safety-Rim Wheels*. You get easy-to-operate, powerful *Safe-Guard Hydraulic Brakes* . . . smoother performance with *Floating Power Engine Mountings* . . . long 117″ Wheelbase—longest in the lowest-priced field.

For slight extra cost—in Special De Luxe models —you get buoyant, restful *Airfoam Seat Cushions*—the latest feature added to the famous Plymouth *Air Pillow Ride.* Only Plymouth has this ride—or anything like it—in the lowest-priced field!

Take a tip from the taxicab operators—*who know from wide experience and accurate records*—there's a lot of *difference* in low-priced cars, and it's Plymouth that makes the difference.

PLYMOUTH BUILDS GREAT CARS...
GOOD SERVICE KEEPS THEM GREAT

Your nearby Plymouth dealer will provide the service and factory-engineered parts to keep your present car in good condition while you're waiting for your new Plymouth.

PLYMOUTH Division of CHRYSLER
CORPORATION, Detroit 31, Michigan

1

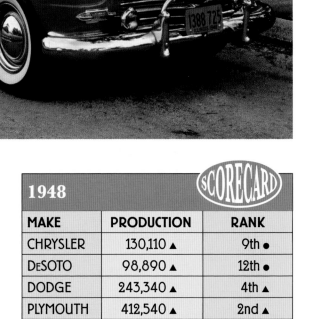

2

1. Plymouth asserted in this ad that more than half of all standard-built cars registered as taxis were Plymouths, and that dependability was the top reason why—which would also make it a great car for you. **2.** Like its Chrysler, DeSoto, and Dodge corporate siblings, Plymouths marched virtually unchanged into 1948 and continued right into 1949's "first series" cars. A Special DeLuxe convertible was the only Chrysler Corporation droptop to retail for less than $2000 in 1948, coming in at $1857.

1948		SCORECARD
MAKE	PRODUCTION	RANK
CHRYSLER	130,110 ▲	9th ●
DeSOTO	98,890 ▲	12th ●
DODGE	243,340 ▲	4th ▲
PLYMOUTH	412,540 ▲	2nd ▲
All figures estimated		

1

2

3

1. Like most Big Three makes, Chrysler Corporation showed its first all-new postwar designs for the 1949 model year, though none arrived until spring. Referred to as the 1949 "second series" (carryover '48s being the "first series" built during the early part of the model year), all four makes had front fenders that flowed into the bodysides but separate rear fenders. At Chrysler, the Town & Country was reduced from two body styles to just a convertible. It carried a unique rear deck and taillights, and wood trim was just an outline this year; the underlying panels were body-colored steel. It listed for a whopping $3970. **2.** By contrast, $3206 bought a New Yorker convertible. Upper-line cars continued with a 135-horsepower 323.5-cubic-inch eight but gained four inches in wheelbase, now at 131.5. **3.** The low-volume, long-wheelbase Crown Imperial returned, now selling for about $5300.

1

2

3

1. Chrysler's lineup again started with the Royal, shown in $2114 club coupe form. **2.** A Chrysler ad explains that building the entire front-end body assembly at one time creates a more solid-feeling car. **3.** By far the most popular "second series" Chrysler was the $2329 Windsor four-door sedan; note the new "stand up" taillights that were fitted to most Chryslers this year. Royals and Windsors kept their 250.6-cubic-inch six, now rated at 116 horsepower, and rode on a 125.5-inch wheelbase, four inches longer than before.

1

2

3

4

1. DeSotos emerged from their 1949 redesign on a four-inch-longer wheelbase, now 125.5 inches, again the same as the six-cylinder Chryslers. The engine remained a 236.6-cubic-inch six, but horsepower jumped by three to 112. DeLuxe and Custom models returned, the latter fielding the lone convertible, priced at $2578. **2-3.** DeSoto's first true station wagon appeared with the redesigned '49s. Placed on a longer 139.5-inch wheelbase, it had a concealed outside spare tire, and the center section of the rear bumper dropped down so the tire could clear it when the tailgate was lowered. The body was all steel with wood trim. **4.** A Custom club coupe listed for $2156.

1. The price leaders of the new **Dodge** lineup were the Wayfarers. The series offered a business coupe, two-door sedan, and two-seat roadster, all on a 115-inch wheelbase—8.5 inches shorter than the company's other '49s. The neat little $1727 roadster was the least-expensive open car offered by the Big Three, partly because it originally came with snap-in side windows and a manually operated top. **2.** The most expensive Wayfarer—and the only one with a rear seat—was the $1738 two-door sedan. **3.** DeLuxe and Custom model names were replaced by Meadowbrook and Coronet for 1949. The former came only as a four-door sedan; the latter included this structural-wood station wagon that sold for $2865. Dodges kept their 230.2-cubic-inch six, now rated at 113 horsepower.

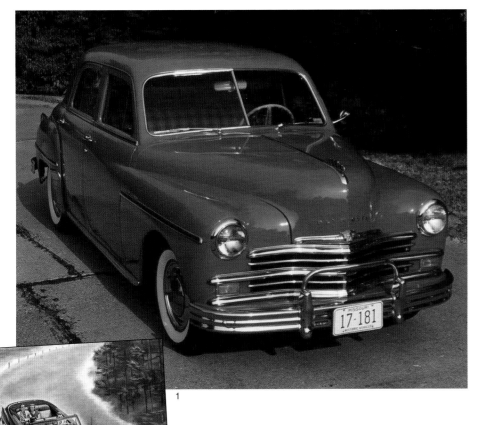

1

2

1. **Plymouth's** redesigned '49s returned in DeLuxe and Special DeLuxe guise on a one-inch-longer wheelbase—now 118.5—but the DeLuxe series included a trio of two-doors on a 111-inch wheelbase. Shown here is the most popular Plymouth, the $1629 Special DeLuxe four-door sedan. 2. Plymouth now offered two wagons, the larger being the wood-sided Special DeLuxe, the most expensive car in the line at $2372. 3. The sharp-looking $1982 Special DeLuxe convertible proved surprisingly popular. 4. So did the "shorty" two-door DeLuxe Suburban wagon, which, at $1840, outsold its four-door "woodie" counterpart by more than five-to-one.

The car that likes to be compared—new Plymouth

3

4

1949		SCORECARD
MAKE	**PRODUCTION**	**RANK**
CHRYSLER	124,218 ▼	12th ▼
DeSOTO	94,201 ▼	14th ▼
DODGE	256,857 ▼	8th ▼
PLYMOUTH	520,385 ▲	3rd ▼
All figures estimated		

Some cars have been likened to appliances, but the Crosley was the product of an appliance company. Powel Crosley, Jr., the radio and refrigerator tycoon, had long dreamed of a simple economy car for the masses. He finally made his move in 1939 with a tiny, stark, two-cylinder job that delivered 50 mpg and cost as little as $290. But the Crosley was a crude curiosity to most Americans, so sales were modest: just 5000 total by the eve of World War II.

After the war came much longer, restyled Crosleys with an unusual copper/sheet-steel four-cylinder engine developed for military use. Horsepower doubled, but the cars were still slow, spartan, and rather dumpy-looking. Worse, the new engine was notoriously unreliable. Still, Crosley thrived in the frantic postwar seller's market, building 53,000 cars for 1946-48, helped by offering a sturdier iron-block engine.

Crosley again restyled for 1949 and added a cute two-seat roadster, the surprising Hotshot. But with buyers flocking to "real" cars in a booming economy, sales started drying up. Crosley tried to turn things around, but the trend was unstoppable. It finally quit the auto business in 1952—proving once again that America still wasn't ready for small cars.

1

2

3

4

1-3. The Crosley debuted for 1939 in convertible coupe (shown) and convertible sedan form. The sole engine was a 35.3-cid, two-cylinder, four-cycle Waukesha that made 12 horsepower. The cars weighed in the neighborhood of 1000 pounds, so 50 mph was possible. The model roster expanded to five body styles for 1940. **4.** The priciest '41 Crosley was the station wagon, which sold for $496.

1

2

1. The postwar Crosley was all-new, larger, more powerful, and more obviously trying to be stylish. The CoBra (for copper-brazed) four churned out 26.5 hp, but the unconventional engine had serious reliability problems. A cast-iron variant soon followed. A 1947 Crosley convertible sedan was just $949, complete with a "roll-top" cloth laminate roof. 2. The 1180-lb Crosley pickup had ¼-ton cargo capacity. Note the fender-mounted antenna for the optional radio on this '47 model. 3. The '49 Crosleys wore more-aggressive front-end sheetmetal. Pictured here, the $866 two-door sedan. 4. The spunky Hotshot roadster (right) debuted for 1949. It was joined for '50 by the Super Sports (left), which boasted better trim and standard doors.

3

4

CROSLEY		SCORECARD
YEAR	PRODUCTION	RANK
1940	422 ▼	20th ●
1941	2,289 ▲	18th ▲
1942	1,029 ▼	18th ●
1946	4,999 ▲	17th ▲
1947	19,344 ▲	19th ▼
1948	26,239 ▲	18th ▲
1949	7,431 ▼	19th ▼

The company that put the world on wheels was teetering on the brink in the late 1940s. Once America's leading automaker by far, Ford was outstripped by General Motors in the late Twenties, then dropped behind Chrysler Corporation in 1936. By the end of World War II, Ford was disorganized and heavily in debt despite fat profits from military contracts. Things were so bad that accountants calculated expenses and income by weighing the paperwork.

This long decline reflected the hidebound attitudes of the irascible Henry Ford, who ruled with an iron hand even after naming son Edsel as company president in 1919. Though the old man scored a last hurrah with his low-priced 1932 Ford V-8, it was Edsel who gave it sales-winning style. Edsel also championed the sleek, affordable Zephyr to help Lincoln cope with a Depression-devastated luxury market and conceived the Mercury brand, which debuted for 1939, as Ford's much-needed contender in the medium-price field. Most of all, he created an undisputed classic in the elegant Zephyr-based Lincoln Continental, which entered production in 1940.

But years of wrangling with the father took a toll on Edsel, and he died at the age of just 49 in 1943. Two years later, the doddering founder finally ceded control to grandson Henry Ford II after prodding by the government. Washington was frankly alarmed by the worsening conditions at Ford, a key defense contractor and major employer.

By the time Old Henry passed on in 1947, the young "HFII" was showing himself to be an able and forceful leader. But everyone knew that salvation rested almost entirely with the all-new 1949 Ford. Though developed in fair haste after a last-minute change of plans, the most-changed Ford since the Model A was no less an instant hit, thus paving the way for even greater Dearborn successes in the expansive 1950s.

3

4

6

5

1. The passing of the torch: The two Henry Fords (pictured here in 1944) study a scale model of their company's sprawling Rouge plant. **2.** A **Ford** Standard Tudor sedan undergoes a headlamp alignment check. Sealed-beam headlamps were a new feature of the 1940 Fords. **3.** The 1940 DeLuxe convertible gained a hydraulically powered top but lost its rumble seat. **4.** This DeLuxe coupe wears optional bumper guards and wheel trim rings. **5.** Ford's 28-millionth car, a 1940 DeLuxe Fordor sedan, appeared at the New York World's Fair. **6.** With a base price of $947, the DeLuxe woodie wagon was the priciest model in Ford's passenger-car lineup.

2

1

3

1. Maintaining a unibody design, the revamped Lincoln Zephyr bodies were wider, taller, and slightly shorter than the previous year. The most popular Lincoln was the $1439 Zephyr four-door sedan. **2.** Under Edsel Ford's direction, designer E. T. "Bob" Gregorie created a true American classic: the Zephyr-based 1940 Continental. The handsome new car debuted as a convertible with an enveloping, cabriolet-style top; later in the model year, it was joined by this coupe. **3-4.** Model-year production of Continentals was limited to 54 coupes and 350 cabriolets; prices were $2783 and $2916, respectively.

4

1

2

1. Mercury styling received a slight freshening for the line's sophomore year. Notable updates included sealed-beam headlights, new taillights, a revised grille, and "Mercury Eight" badging. Engineering improvements included better hydraulic brakes, improved shocks, and a torsion-bar ride stabilizer. The hardtop-like "sedan coupe" boasted roll-down rear windows and started at $987. **2.** The ragtop coupe started at $1079. **3.** The Mercury roster grew by one model this year, as a new convertible sedan body style joined the lineup. But phaeton-style cars were fast falling out of favor; Mercury produced just 979 convertible sedans for 1940, and dropped the model after just one year.

3

1940	SCORECARD	
MAKE	**PRODUCTION**	**RANK**
FORD	541,896 ▲	2nd ●
LINCOLN	21,765 ▲	16th ▼
MERCURY	81,128* ▲	12th ▼
*figure estimated		

2

3

4

5

1

1. The Ford model lineup was revised to encompass three price levels (Special, DeLuxe, and Super DeLuxe) offered in two series (Six and V-8). The $1013 Super DeLuxe wagon was the first Ford to surpass $1000 since the 1930 Model A Town Car. **2.** New front and rear styling introduced a "square box" look, as seen on this Super DeLuxe club coupe. **3.** The $807 Super DeLuxe five-passenger coupe was also known as an "opera" coupe because of its folding rear seats. **4.** Chrome fender strips, as seen on this $950 Super DeLuxe ragtop, were a midyear addition. **5.** Ford's best-seller for 1941 was the Super DeLuxe Tudor sedan. Six and V-8 sales of this model totaled more than 185,000 cars.

1

2

3

1. The Lincoln Zephyr line saw minor changes for 1941, among them slightly revised grilles and relocated parking lights. **2.** At $1858, the most-expensive Zephyr was the convertible coupe. Only 725 were built. All Lincoln convertibles now had electric-powered tops instead of vacuum assist. **3.** The Zephyr club coupe sported a new fold-down rear-seat center armrest. With a production run of 3750, the club coupe was the second-most-popular Lincoln, trailing the Zephyr sedan.

1

1-2. "Lincoln Continental" script appeared for the first time on the mildly changed Continental, which now had its own series. All Continentals shared the Zephyr's 125-inch wheelbase and 120-hp, 292-cid V-12 engine. 3. Production of the $2812 club coupes totaled just 850, and only 400 cabriolets were built. 4. Continental interiors offered plush accommodations, including gold-toned trim. Rectangular gauges were replaced with round instrumentation this year.

3

2

4

1

2

3

1. Like their Ford cousins, **Mercurys** were redesigned on a two-inch-longer wheelbase with boxier styling. Mercury's best-seller was the four-door or "town" sedan. Priced at $987, it was the last Merc four-door that would sell for less than $1000.
2. Convertibles were priced at $1100. 3. Mercury's 239.4-cid flathead V-8 received a five-horsepower bump, to an even 100. This splashy ad is evidence of the aviation world's growing influence on automotive marketing and design in the 1940s.

1

2

1. Fords got a new front end with one-piece fenders and a fully horizontal grille. The Super DeLuxe station wagon remained the most-expensive Ford at $1115 with the flathead six or $1125 with the eight. **2.** Only 2920 Super DeLuxe convertibles were produced before civilian car production was halted on February 10. **3.** DeLuxe series cars, like this Fordor sedan, had painted grille surrounds and "DeLuxe" spelled out vertically in the center grille bar. **4.** The Super DeLuxe Fordor in this publicity photo was too nicely equipped for military service. A dechromed Special Fordor proved to be the War Department Ford of choice for use at U.S. bases.

3

4

1

2

3

4

1. Heavy, squarish styling in the Cadillac mode became the new look for **Lincoln** in 1942. It was carried on all three series offered that year: Custom, Continental, and Zephyr. Shown here are the $1700 Zephyr club coupe (left) and the $1650 three-window coupe. **2.** At $3075, the Custom limousine was the most-expensive Lincoln for '42. **3.** A new top design that permitted roll-down rear windows was the most significant upgrade to the Zephyr convertible coupe. The rarest of all Lincolns this year, a mere 191 were built. **4.** The final '42 Lincoln rolled off the assembly line on January 31, 1942.

1

2

1. Partly in response to Cadillac's move to bolder front-end design, Continental's softly contoured grille was given a heavier-looking, more-upright treatment shared with other Lincolns. Power windows and front-seat adjustors became standard. Only 136 cabriolets were built, compared to 200 club coupes. **2.** Known as the "Sunshine Special," president Franklin Delano Roosevelt's 1939 K Series was shipped to Detroit to be updated and armor plated. Lincoln replaced the front end with '42-style fenders and grille, and added 17-inch wheels.

1

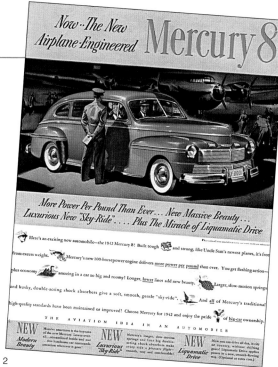

2

4

3

1. The facelifted 1942 **Mercurys** got a Lincolnesque look via a new split-horizontal grille and more-massive front fenders. The base price of the station wagon crept up $119 to $1260 this year. **2.** This ad depicts Mercury's most-popular '42 model, the $1065 four-door Town Sedan. It saw sales of 10,475. **3.** Mercury dashboards got a new symmetrical look, with speedometer and clock gauges flanking a central speaker grille. **4.** World War II production demands helped limit output of the $1030 two-door sedan to just 4820 units. Note the dual chrome fender strips, a new Mercury styling feature.

1942		SCORECARD
MAKE	**PRODUCTION**	**RANK**
FORD	160,432 ▼	2nd ●
LINCOLN	6,567 ▼	17th ▼
MERCURY	22,816 ▼	14th ▼

1946

1

2

3

4

1. Ford got postwar production underway on July 3, 1945, the first automaker to do so. Many early cars were sent to police departments and other fleets. The '46s were mildly facelifted '42s, the new horizontal bar grille being the main giveaway. **2.** The six-passenger sedan coupe came only in top-rung Super DeLuxe trim, priced at $1307 with V-8 power. Few shoppers were interested in front-seat-only business coupes after the war. **3-4.** Introduced midyear as the most-expensive Ford, the Sportsman convertible coupe sold for $1982. While steel remained in short supply, wood for the Sportsman was abundant in Ford's forests near Iron Mountain, Michigan. To build the car, solid wood blocks were hand cut, fitted, and varnished. The high price and maintenance required by the wood panels meant low sales numbers; only 1209 Sportsmans left showroom floors in its inaugural year.

1

2

1. As the war went, so did the Zephyr name. Lincoln's least-expensive offering was now known simply as the club coupe. All Lincolns wore heavier-looking front bumpers and a new eggcrate-style grille this year. **2.** Very early 1946 Lincolns, like this four-door sedan, lacked road lamps built in to the far ends of the lower grille. **3-4.** Lincoln Continental output totaled a modest 201 cabriolets and 265 club coupes. Henry Ford II paced the 1946 Indianapolis 500 in a special yellow cabriolet.

3

4

1

2

3

4

1. The one-year-only **Mercury** Sportsman shared its body and woodwork with Ford's similar, but less-expensive, Sportsman. The costliest '46 Merc at $2209, only 205 were sold. **2.** The '46 Mercurys were essentially '42 models with new grilles, hoods, and trim. A station wagon sold for $1788. **3.** The most-popular Merc two-door was the sedan-coupe; 24,163 were sold. **4.** This station wagon was outfitted for camping with a Marmon-Herrington 4×4 conversion.

1946 SCORECARD		
MAKE	PRODUCTION	RANK
FORD	468,022 ▲	1st ▲
LINCOLN	16,645 ▲	16th ▲
MERCURY	86,608 ▲	10th ▲

2

1. The 1947 **Fords** wore a minor facelift with slightly different grilles and trim. The parking lights migrated from above the grille to below the headlights. 2. The wood-bodied Sportsman convertible returned for '47, and its sales crept up slightly to 2282. This example wears accessory fog lights, spotlights, and fender skirts. 3. Available only in Super DeLuxe trim, the sedan coupe stickered for $1409 with the V-8 engine. 4. Woodie wagons remained a part of the Ford lineup, all wearing Super DeLuxe trim. Pricing started at $1972 with a V-8, or $1893 with a six.

3

4

1947

3

1

BABE RUTH
OFFICIAL CAR

4

2

5

6

8

7

9

10

1-2. Almost unchanged, the Lincoln Continental returned with an asking price of $4662. 3. Priced about $2000 less than a Continental coupe, the $2533 Lincoln club coupe soldiered on as the make's price leader. 4. Continentals were popular with celebrities. This cabriolet proved to be a worthy conveyance for baseball legend Babe Ruth (rear center). 5. Lincoln sedans started at $2554, but an optional interior upgrade package added $168 to the tab. 6-7. Keeping in step with other Ford Motor Company cars, the 1947 Mercurys received only slightly different grilles and trim. The $1645 sedan coupe found 29,284 takers. 8-10. Club convertible buyers had a choice of red or tan interior upholstery. The little-changed ragtop rolled on with an asking price of $2002. The "waterfall" grille design would be a Mercury styling point for the next few years.

1947		SCORECARD
MAKE	PRODUCTION	RANK
FORD	429,674 ▼	2nd ▼
LINCOLN	21,460 ▲	18th ▼
MERCURY	85,383 ▼	13th ▼

1

3

2

4

1. Awaiting the all-new 1949 models, '48 **Fords** were virtually unchanged. Unlike most other manufacturers, Ford held the line on prices this year. A Super DeLuxe V-8 Fordor sedan listed for $1440, the same as in '47. **2.** The four-door-only woodie wagon would be replaced by a two-door-only partial woodie for 1949-51. **3-4.** The sedan coupe was the third-most-popular Super DeLuxe model, with sales of 70,826. **5.** The Super DeLuxe convertible went for $1740, also the same as in '47.

5

1. With redesigned 1949 models on the way, the '48 Lincolns stood pat. This was the swan song year for both the Continental and Lincoln's V-12 engine. **2.** The convertible was the heaviest model in the Lincoln line, weighing in at a little more than 4200 pounds. **3.** Continental cabriolet output slipped to 452, while coupe sales increased slightly to 847. **4.** The four-door sedan accounted for approximately 4800 of the year's 7769 Lincolns and Continentals.

2

1

3

4

1

2

1. Like their corporate kin, the 1948 Mercurys were carried over in anticipation of all-new 1949 models. Here, the $2002 convertible. **2.** The most popular of the '48 Mercs was the $1660 four-door town sedan. **3.** Mercury interiors were subtly two-toned. **4.** The $2207 station wagon saw output drop to 1889 units. This one served as an ambulance in Detroit for Lincoln-Mercury's medical department.

3

4

1948		*Scorecard*
MAKE	**PRODUCTION**	**RANK**
FORD	247,722 ▼	3rd ▼
LINCOLN	7,769 ▼	19th ▼
MERCURY	50,268 ▼	16th ▼

1949

1. Ford introduced its redesigned '49s in June 1948, with a gala unveiling at the Waldorf-Astoria Hotel in New York. A revolving turntable highlighted five Custom models: Fordor, station wagon, Tudor, convertible, and club coupe. Preview visitors could gape at Ford's flush-fender body and inspect the underside. Except on convertibles, the X-member chassis was gone, replaced by a ladder-type frame. **2.** Ford brothers Benson and Henry II (left and center) chat with corporate management whiz Ernest Breech (right) at the introduction of the new Ford lineup. **3.** Showgoers swarm the new Ford during its unveiling. Ford executives were most certainly relieved at the warm public reception, as the success of the '49 lineup was crucial to the survival of the company.

1

2

3

1

2

3

4

6

5

1-4. Slab sided in profile, three inches lower, slightly shorter and narrower, the '49 Ford marked a dramatic change from prior models. The Custom V-8 convertible listed for $1886, the club coupe $1511. **5.** Unlike previous Ford wagons, the new '49 had an all-steel body overlaid with molded plywood paneling—none of the wood was structural. **6.** Standard Fords were more austere than their Custom kin. Here, a Standard Tudor sedan outfitted for police duty. **7.** The Custom Fordor sedan cost $1559.
8. William, Benson, and Henry Ford II celebrate the one-millionth Ford built for '49.

7

8

MILLIONTH 49 FORD

2

3

4

5

6

1. The redesigned 1949 **Lincolns** wore new bodies with flow-through fenders. Base models shared body components with Mercury and rode a 121-inch wheelbase, while uplevel Cosmopolitan models had exclusive bodies on a 125-inch wheelbase. Replacing the Lincoln V-12 was a 337-cid, 152-hp flathead V-8. Base four-door sedans like this one started at $2575. **2-3.** Lincoln offered two different four-door sedans in the Cosmopolitan lineup, both with a $3238 price tag. The sport sedan wore a notchback roofline. The town sedan (shown here) sported an unpopular fastback roofline, and it was discontinued before the year was out. All four-door sedans retained the rear-hinged "suicide" doors of their predecessors. **4-5.** For buyers who didn't want to step up to the $3948 Cosmopolitan convertible, Lincoln offered this $3116 base ragtop. **6.** A Lincoln Cosmopolitan sport sedan was chosen as the basis for a stretched Presidential limousine. Note the continental kit and stretched rear bumper, duplicate "eyebrow" trim over the rear wheel well, and clear roof section mounted over the stacked convertible top.

1. The redesigned '49 **Mercurys** wore curvaceous new bodies, most of which were shared with lower-line Lincolns. The $2410 convertible accounted for 16,765 sales. **2.** Though it shared its two-door body with Ford, the Mercury station wagon still rode a four-inch-longer wheelbase. Compared with the rest of the line, the wagon was a slow seller, with only 8044 finding homes. **3.** Mercury's new cars helped sales increase sixfold over 1948. The best-selling model was the $2031 four-door sport sedan, pictured here with an optional sun shade. **4.** The least-expensive Mercury was the $1979 club coupe. It quickly became a favorite of Fifties customizers, who swapped trim pieces, lowered suspensions, and "chopped" tops to personalize their cars.

1949		SCORECARD
MAKE	PRODUCTION	RANK
FORD	1,118,308 ▲	1st ▲
LINCOLN	73,507 ▲	17th ▲
MERCURY	301,319 ▲	6th ▲

1. Female workers assemble aircraft wings at Chrysler's Jefferson Ave. plant in Detroit. 2. With a "ceiling" spec of nearly 32,000 feet, a B-29 Superfortress needed four 2200-horsepower Wright Duplex Cyclone engines, many of which Chrysler manufactured. The Cyclone was an 18-cylinder radial fitted with a pair of exhaust-driven turbochargers. 3. Nash-Kelvinator made props, aircraft engines, Sikorsky helicopters, binoculars, and more. 4. Hudson, which would create wonderfully innovative cars postwar, did its bit with precision manufacture of aircraft pistons. Note the bright fluorescent lighting, a must for quality control.

1

3

2

1. Workers at the enormous new Ford factory at Willow Run, near Detroit, had turned out 8675 B-24 Liberator bombers before the plant closed in 1945. At its peak in summer 1944, the factory was capable of cranking out one bomber every hour. **2.** Hudson electricians carefully wire B-29 bombers. **3.** Studebaker manufactured Wright R-1820 Cyclone engines under license for the B-17 Flying Fortress. Patriotic ads gave automakers valuable exposure during a period when new autos weren't available.

1943-45

1. General Douglas MacArthur takes a jeep tour of blasted Corregidor, a small island in the Philippines, in March 1945. American soldiers cherished their jeeps for their incredible durability and go-anywhere, do-anything capability. Army chief of staff General George Marshall called the jeep "America's greatest contribution to modern warfare." **2.** Jeeps underwent many running design changes throughout the course of the war. High ground clearance aided off-loading into water, as this early-model Willys demonstrates. Combined, Ford and Willys had built well over a half-million jeeps by the war's end.

1

2

1. Studebaker brags on its Weasel personnel and cargo carrier and on the company's role in the production of Wright engines used by the B-17. **2.** GM's Truck and Coach division developed the hardy "Duck," an amphibious craft that saw combat duty around the globe. Shown here (from left to right) are the 8-ton, 4-ton, and 2-ton models. A much smaller Marmon-Herrington variant was dubbed the "Seep."

1

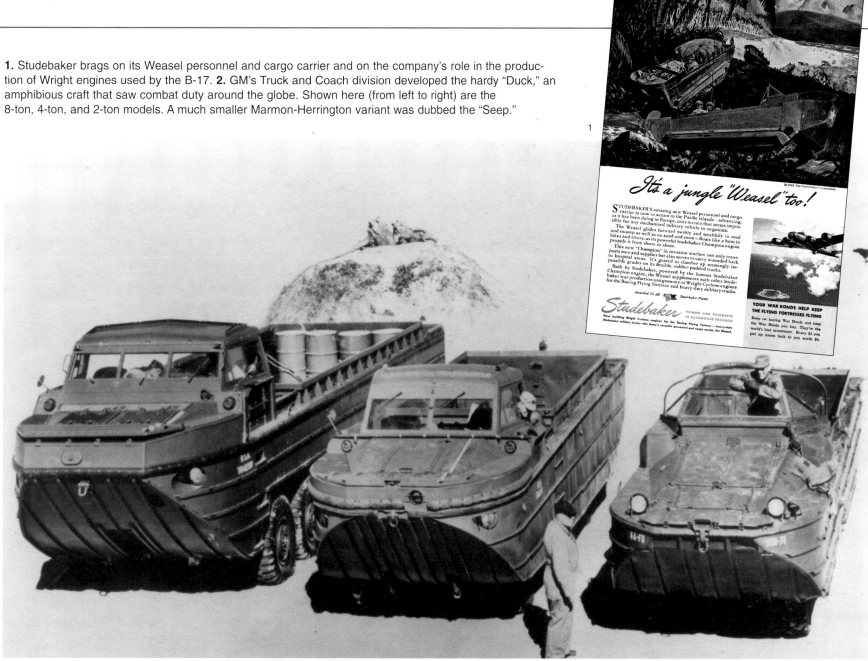

2

Success often breeds success, and so it was with General Motors in the 1940s. Having surpassed Ford Motor Company as America's largest automaker in the 1930s, GM continued to prosper with consistently appealing products created and sold by some of the most talented executives anywhere. Increasing size brought increased pricing power, allowing GM to undercut rivals and still earn healthy profits—which only fueled further growth. By decade's end, GM was the largest company the world had ever seen and the undisputed industry pacesetter for styling, engineering, and marketing.

Astute timing was another key to GM's success. For example, the "junior Cadillac" LaSalle was dropped after 1940 because it was no longer needed. GM's five remaining makes restyled for 1941-42, and thus seemed quite fresh when they returned to production

after World War II. For 1948 came redesigned Oldsmobiles and Cadillacs with aircraft-inspired styling that proved both influential and popular. The following year, GM introduced America's first modern high-compression V-8 engines, a perfect match for its pioneering fully automatic Hydra-Matic transmission, plus the "hardtop convertible" body style that would sweep Detroit in the Fifties. All-new Buicks, Chevrolets, and Pontiacs completed the knockout '49 corporate lineup and a historic GM decade.

1. On January 11, 1940, William "Big Bill" Knudsen (at microphone), GM president since 1937, heralds the corporation's 25-millionth passenger car, a 1940 Chevrolet Master DeLuxe Town Sedan. At his right is M. E. Coyle, Chevy president since 1933. To Knudsen's left are GM chairman Alfred P. Sloan, Jr. and, to his left, Charles "Engine Charlie" Wilson.

2

1. The 1940 **Buicks** got an updated look via a new grille and fenders. The $996 four-door sedan was the most-popular model in the entry-level Special series, with a production run of 68,816. **2.** This Special four-door sedan is painted Ludington Green and is equipped with the ultrarare factory sunroof. Sidemount spare tires were fast becoming passé. **3.** The rarest Special this year was the $1355 sport phaeton. Only 597 were built. **4.** All Buick Special and Super models rode a 121-inch wheelbase. At $895, the Special business coupe was the lowest-priced car in Buick's stable for 1940.

1

3

4

1. The 1940 Buicks looked especially handsome in coupe form. Here, the $1058 Super Sport Coupe in Royal Maroon. 2. This advertisement touts the Buick Townmaster Sedan, a custom-built town car with bodywork by the Brunn Co. of Buffalo, NY. It was built on the standard 126-inch-wheelbase Roadmaster chassis. 3. Buick's first station wagon, the wood-bodied Estate Wagon, was available only in the new-for-1940 Super series. Pricing for Buick's woodie started at $1242, and production totaled only 501 units. 4. With sales of 4802, the most popular of Buick's convertible coupes was the $1211 Super ragtop. Specials and Supers used the smaller of Buick's two straight eights, a 248-cubic-incher that was rated at 107 horsepower. 5. At the top of Buick's lineup stood the Series 80 and Series 90 Limited models. Series 80 Limiteds, like this sport phaeton, rode on a 133-inch wheelbase. Series 90 cars used a 140-inch span. Century, Roadmaster, and Limited models used Buick's 141-horsepower, 320.2-cubic-inch straight eight.

1

2

3

1. Cadillac's new Series 62 rode on a 129-inch wheelbase, three inches longer than the Series 61 it replaced. This dashing convertible wears custom bodywork by coachbuilding firm Bohman and Schwartz. **2.** The Sixty-Special sedan, Cadillac's style leader, returned with only minor styling tweaks. A predictive (if rarely ordered) option was a sliding metal sunroof, called the "Sunshine Turret Top Roof." **3.** Though 1940 was the marque's last year, **LaSalle** wasn't about to go out quietly. Modified styling was a high point, plus, for the first time in more than a decade, models were available in two series. The design leader was the plush new Series 52 Special lineup, which bore Harley Earl's latest "torpedo" look. A total of 10,250 Series 52 Special four-door sedans were sold, making it the best-selling LaSalle. **4.** Series 52 LaSalles, like this four-door convertible sedan, shared Cadillac's sleek C-body. Series 50 models used Buick's B-body. **5.** The elegant Series 52 convertible coupe started at $1535. All 1940 LaSalles used a 130-horsepower, 322-cubic-inch L-head V-8.

4

5

1

2

3

4

1. For **Chevrolet**, 1940 brought some notable changes, including "Royal Clipper" styling that boasted more-flowing lines and Buick-like grilles. The convertible was offered only in the new top-line Special DeLuxe series. 2. The Master DeLuxe business coupe had an open luggage area behind the front seat; sport coupes had a rear bench seat. 3. The Special DeLuxe town sedan was the year's top-selling Chevy at 205,910 units. 4. A four-door sport sedan was a new body style for 1940. This Master DeLuxe model tallied 40,924 orders. 5. Chevrolet's priciest offering for 1940 was the $934 Special DeLuxe woodie wagon. 6. The best-selling 1940 **Oldsmobile** was the $1131 Series 90 four-door sedan.

5

6

1

2

3

4

1. Oldsmobile's big news for 1940 was Hydra-Matic, the industry's first truly automatic transmission. Olds was eager to show that Hydra-Matic eliminated the clutch pedal, as this PR photo attests. 2. The Custom Cruiser designation made its debut on Series 90s, all of which ran a 257-cubic-inch 110-horse inline eight-cylinder engine and featured the Cadillac C-body. Here, a $1069 Series 90 club coupe. 3. Comprised of a white ash frame with walnut-finished birch panels, Olds's woodie body was built by Hercules Body Co. All wagons offered special heavy-duty rear coil springs to carry heavy loads. 4. The 1940 Oldsmobiles had a wider grille and front fenders, plus semi-integrated headlights. 5. **Pontiacs** also received a facelift with new grilles and semi-integrated headlights. This Special six four-door sedan started at $876. 6. The $25,000 Plexiglas Pontiac promotional car, a DeLuxe Six four-door sedan, showed "at a glance the hidden value built into Pontiac cars."

5

6

1940

2

1

3

1. Pontiac's Special Six two-door touring sedan was based on Chevrolet's A-body and rode a 117-inch wheelbase. **2.** All Pontiac interiors were trimmed with grained Continental Walnut. **3.** The Special Six woodie station wagon sold for $1015 and came standard with a fender-mounted spare tire. Special and DeLuxe Six models used a 223-cubic-inch 87-horsepower inline six-cylinder engine. **4.** All Pontiac Torpedo Eights, such as this four-door sedan, used Cadillac's C-body on a 122-inch wheelbase.

4

1940		SCORECARD
MAKE	**PRODUCTION**	**RANK**
BUICK	278,784 ▲	4th ●
CADILLAC	13,043 ▼	18th ●
CHEVROLET	764,616 ▲	1st ●
LaSALLE	24,130 ▲	15th ▲
OLDSMOBILE	185,154 ▲	7th ●
PONTIAC	217,001 ▲	5th ▲

2

3

1

1. **Buick's** best-selling convertible, at 12,391 units, was the Series 50 Super. 2. The Super and Roadmaster lines had the last convertible phaetons Buick would ever offer. The $1555 Super is shown. 3. The most-popular Super model, the $1185 four-door sedan, saw sales of 58,638. 4. The dazzling Super dashboards featured engine-turned metal panels flanking a central radio speaker. 5. All Centurys had Compound Carburetion, which helped boost the horsepower of the "Fireball 8" to 165.

4

5

1

1. The '41 **Cadillacs** introduced the rectangular eggcrate grille that would become the make's trademark. The Series 62 convertible coupe outsold its convertible-sedan counterpart almost eight-to-one. **2.** Sixty Specials lacked running boards and the chrome strips found on the fenders of other '41 Cadillacs. Sixty Specials listed at $2195 or $2395 with a "formal" glass division. **3.** The new Series 63, which was only offered as a four-door sedan, filled the price void between the Series 62 below it and the Sixty Special above it. **4.** Convertible sedans were fading fast industrywide, and 1941 was the final year for Cadillac's version. Just 400 were built.

2

3

4

1. Accessory chrome-trim items could gussy up a value-leader **Chevy**. This Special DeLuxe convertible coupe wears optional fog lamps, stainless-steel fender trim, bumper wing guards, and an accessory hood ornament. 2. Chevrolet's second redesign in as many years stretched the wheelbase to 116 inches, concealed the running boards, incorporated the headlights into the fenders, and gave the front and rear windows a greater slope. 3. White ash and mahogany woodie station wagon bodies were supplied by Cantrell or Ionia Manufacturing. Only available in Special DeLuxe trim, the $995 wagon was the costliest of all 1941 Chevrolets. 4. Based on the Master DeLuxe business coupe, Chevy's coupe pickup used an abbreviated load bed that slotted into the trunk opening.

1. The 1941 **Oldsmobiles** featured new styling touches such as inboard headlights and hidden running boards. Convertibles used a cabriolet-style roof. **2.** The "torpedo" bodies ushered in for 1940 were updated and used on cars like the 98 Custom Cruiser four-door sedan. **3.** The Dynamic Cruiser four-door sedan wore sleek fastback styling. **4.** Priced at $1575, the 98 convertible sedan was the most expensive '41 Oldsmobile. **5.** The entry-level series in the 1941 Oldsmobile lineup was the Series 60 Special. Olds made 31,010 of these Special four-door sedans—25,125 with six-cylinder engines and 3885 with eights.

1

2

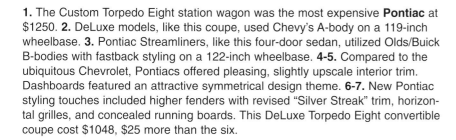

3

4

5

1. The Custom Torpedo Eight station wagon was the most expensive **Pontiac** at $1250. **2.** DeLuxe models, like this coupe, used Chevy's A-body on a 119-inch wheelbase. **3.** Pontiac Streamliners, like this four-door sedan, utilized Olds/Buick B-bodies with fastback styling on a 122-inch wheelbase. **4-5.** Compared to the ubiquitous Chevrolet, Pontiacs offered pleasing, slightly upscale interior trim. Dashboards featured an attractive symmetrical design theme. **6-7.** New Pontiac styling touches included higher fenders with revised "Silver Streak" trim, horizontal grilles, and concealed running boards. This DeLuxe Torpedo Eight convertible coupe cost $1048, $25 more than the six.

6

7

1941		SCORECARD
MAKE	PRODUCTION	RANK
BUICK	374,196 ▲	4th ●
CADILLAC	66,130 ▲	15th ▲
CHEVROLET	1,008,976 ▲	1st ●
OLDSMOBILE	265,864 ▲	6th ▲
PONTIAC	330,061 ▲	5th ●

1

2

3

1. New styling brought the **Buick** Super four-door sedan's front fenders into the doors. **2.** Super and Roadmaster two-door models featured sweptback, or "Airfoil," fenders that flowed all the way into the rear fenders. Here, the $1230 sedanet. **3.** Estate Wagons were among the rarest '42 Buicks, with only 327 produced during the shortened model year. **4-5.** Buick offered convertible coupes in the Special, Super, and Roadmaster series. The entry-level Special (shown here) started at $1260 and saw a production run of 1788.

4

5

1. The regal Series 75 was the only **Cadillac** to maintain squared-off fenders with three-bar chrome trim. **2.** The Series 61 coupe was the lowest priced Cadillac at $1450. **3. Chevy's** Fleetline Aerosedan was as much an instant hit as the fastbacks introduced by General Motors' senior makes for '41. **4.** Chevrolet Fleetlines had Cadillac-inspired chrome fender "speedlines." **5.** Chevy's Special DeLuxe Sport Sedan tallied 31,441 sales in the war-shortened model year.

1

2

3

4

1. A mere 1972 Chevrolet Special DeLuxe cabriolets were built before car production ended on February 9, 1942. **2.** This ad touts Chevrolet's styling, performance, and economy, as well as the company's contribution to the war effort. **3.** This Fleetline Sportmaster sedan was restored as a military staff car, but all that chrome would have been inappropriate—and mostly likely unavailable—on a military vehicle. **4.** After the entrance into World War II, the U.S. government placed restrictions on stainless-steel and chrome trim, as this Special DeLuxe Fleetline "blackout special" displays.

1. Hydra-Matic was still a selling point, but military efforts crept into almost all 1942 **Oldsmobile** ads. The "B-44" designation denoted the division's 44 years in business. **2.** The 98 line was down to three models, including this four-door sedan. **3-4.** New styling included a two-tier bumper/grille, as seen here on the $1020 Special 66 two-door sedan and $1015 club coupe. **5.** A "blackout special" 98 club sedan was the last Olds built before conversion to war production.

1

2

3

1. Pontoon-style fenders extended into the doors of the 1942 **Pontiacs**. **2.** Pontiacs were wider, heavier, and longer this year. The grilles, although running the width of the car, had a vertical center section that mimicked the hood line. **3.** The Torpedo Six four-door sedan started at $985. **4.** Like all General Motors ads of the day, Pontiac advertisements noted quality in unsure times and promoted the company's war effort.

1942		SCORECARD
MAKE	**PRODUCTION**	**RANK**
BUICK	92,573 ▼	4th ●
CADILLAC	16,511 ▼	15th ●
CHEVROLET	254,885 ▼	1st ●
OLDSMOBILE	67,783 ▼	7th ▼
PONTIAC	83,555 ▼	5th ●

1

... so nice to come home to !

BUICK WILL BUILD THEM

BUICK DIVISION OF **GENERAL MOTORS**

2

4

3

1. Substantially redesigned for 1942, the 1946 **Buicks** looked fresher than most competitors. The '46s had less trim and a revised grille. The new "bombsight" hood ornament became a popular aftermarket item. **2.** This 1945 ad anticipated the end of the war while showing off a 1942 Roadmaster ragtop. **3.** "Airfoil" fenders now stretched the length of four-door models. Here, the $2110 Roadmaster sedan. **4.** The 248-cubic-inch straight eight returned in Supers and Specials, still rated at 110 horsepower. The Super convertible started at $2046.

1

2

1. Cadillac Series 62 dashboards reverted to the 1941 style with round gauges instead of rectangular as in 1942. **2.** The Series 62 Club Coupe, with its fastback styling, returned, but not until a few months into production. Grille changes were minimal—the parking lights became rectangular instead of round, and the bars were slightly heavier

3

and spread further apart. The front and rear bumpers now wrapped further around the body. **3.** The familiar Cadillac "V" emblem appeared with the crest on the hood and trunk for the first time. **4.** This Series 62 Club Coupe has the early production rubber rear fender guards. They were replaced with chrome units as a running change during the year. This model started at $2284.

4

1

3

2

4

1. The $1250 **Chevrolet** Fleetmaster four-door sport sedan was the division's second-best seller in 1946. **2.** The popular Chevy Fleetline Aerosedan started at $1249. **3.** The rarest and most expensive 1946 **Oldsmobile** was the 98 convertible. Priced at $2040, only 875 were sold. **4.** Olds Custom Cruiser 98 mechanicals were unchanged from prewar models: a 127-inch wheelbase with a 257-cid, 110-hp straight-eight engine.

1

2

3

4

1. This lavish 1946 Oldsmobile display included a 1942 four-door sedan equipped with Olds's "Valiant" control system for people with physical infirmities, especially disabled veterans. 2. Pontiac wasn't really "new" for 1946. Save for a few minor improvements, the cars were basically reissued '42s. 3. The Pontiac Torpedo Eight sedan coupe started at $1428. This example wears non-stock hubcaps. 4. The Streamliner eight-passenger woodie station wagon started at $1942 with six-cylinder power, or $1970 with an eight.

1946		SCORECARD
MAKE	PRODUCTION	RANK
BUICK	153,627 ▲	5th ▼
CADILLAC	29,214 ▲	14th ▲
CHEVROLET	398,028 ▲	2nd ▼
OLDSMOBILE	117,623 ▲	7th ●
PONTIAC	137,640 ▼	6th ▼

1

2

3

4

1-2. The 1947 **Buicks** were basically '46s with new grilles. Attractive two-tone paint was an extra-cost option on all Buicks. The Roadmaster sedanet listed at $2131, an increase of $117 from the year before. Still, production more than doubled, to 19,212 units. **3.** Buick convertibles, such as this Roadmaster, had hydraulic-assist tops. **4.** Priced at $1929, the Super four-door sedan was the most popular '47 Buick, selling 83,576 units. Buick's straight-eight engines remained the same: Specials and Supers had 248 cubic inches and 110 horsepower, while Roadmasters had 320 cubes and 144 horses.

2

3

1

4

1. **Cadillacs** got minor trim changes and a new grille for '47. The only ragtop in the lineup was the Series 62 convertible, priced at $2902. **2.** The Series 62 two-door coupe accounted for only 4764 sales. **3. Chevrolets** also got a new grille and trim updates this year. Sales of the Fleetline Sportmaster four-door sedan increased from 7501 to 54,531 units. **4.** More than 750 Chevrolet dealers paraded through the streets of Flint, Michigan, to celebrate the opening of the town's new Chevy assembly plant.

1

2

3

1. The Fleetmaster convertible remained Chevy's glamour queen for 1947. 2. A record 28,443 ragtops rolled off Chevy's assembly lines this year. This example wears the Country Club wood trim kit offered by Engineered Enterprises of Detroit. 3. This Fleetmaster coupe is outfitted with several period accessories including rear fender skirts, spotlamp, and a windshield visor. 4. Chevy dealers were able to move more than 159,000 Fleetline Aerosedans off their lots.

4

1

1. The 1947 **Oldsmobile** dashboard was little changed from Olds's prewar design. **2.** Priced at $1433, the two-door club sedan was the most popular Series 66 Special; a total of 23,960 were sold. **3.** From the exterior, the only way to tell a '47 Olds from a '46 was the chrome spear on each front door and fender. The inset with the "Oldsmobile" lettering on the '47 version was larger. For $121 more than a Series 66 club sedan, buyers could step up to an eight-cylinder Dynamic Cruiser 78 version, like this one.

2

3

1

1-2. Accessories on this **Pontiac** Torpedo Eight convertible coupe include turn signals, fender skirts, bumper wing guards, and the optional radio. **3.** The Streamliner Eight wagon went for $2282 in basic form or $2359 as a DeLuxe. **4.** Streamliners used GM's B-body and had moldings around the side windows, while the smaller Torpedoes had beltline moldings. The handsome Streamliner sedan coupe went for $1547 with a six or $1595 with an eight.

2

3

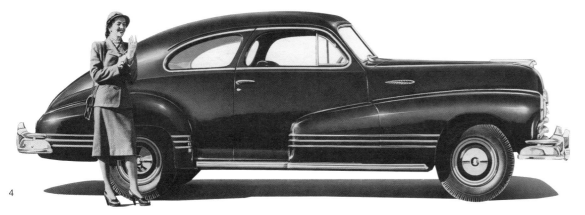

4

1947		SCORECARD
MAKE	**PRODUCTION**	**RANK**
BUICK	272,827 ▲	4th ▲
CADILLAC	61,926 ▲	16th ▼
CHEVROLET	671,546 ▲	1st ▲
OLDSMOBILE	193,895 ▲	7th ●
PONTIAC	230,600 ▲	6th ●

4

1

1. Buick's big news for '48 was the Dynaflow automatic transmission, introduced as a $244 option on Roadmasters. Dynaflow used a hydraulic torque convertor and wasn't as efficient as the Olds and Cadillac Hydra-Matic. **2.** Buick again sold more convertibles than any other automaker—more than 30,000 this year. **3.** Luxurious Roadmaster interiors included power windows and leather seats. **4.** The $3734 Roadmaster Estate Wagon drew only 350 orders. **5.** The $3127 Super Estate Wagon did better, finding 2018 buyers.

2

3

5

1

2

3

1. Cadillacs got a total redesign, complete with tailfins inspired by the P-38 Lightning fighter plane. These were among the first all-new postwar cars from a big-three automaker. **2.** At $2728, the Series 61 club coupe, or Sedanet, was the least costly '48 Caddy. Many fans consider it the prettiest postwar American fastback. **3.** The Series 62 convertible continued as Cadillac's lone ragtop. The bright stone shields behind the front tires, rocker moldings, and the three chrome strips beneath the taillights were Series 62-exclusive trim pieces. **4.** GM vice president M. E. Coyle posed with this sign comparing the 1948 **Chevrolet** to a 1929 Buick. Why the seemingly odd match-up? To "prove" GM was offering more car for the money than it had 20 years before.

4

1

2

3

4

5

1. Part of the Chevy Fleetline Sportmaster sedan's appeal was its similarity to GM's senior line cars. Sales increased 18 percent over '47, but it was still outsold by the Aerosedan by more than three to one. **2.** Convertible sales were down 28 percent to 20,471. **3.** The Fleetmaster woodie wagon started at $2013. **4.** The Fleetline two-door Aerosedan was Chevy's most-popular car, selling more than 211,000 units. Prices started at $1434. **5.** The five-passenger sport coupe was the only Fleetmaster coupe; the entry-level Stylemaster lineup offered a business coupe as well.

1

2

3

4

6

5

1. The Futuramic 98 **Oldsmobiles**, introduced in February '48, represented "the dramatic design of the future." **2.** The 98 club sedan sported fastback styling, which would soon wane in popularity. **3.** The third of three 98 body styles was this convertible. The Futuramic 98 proved very popular; 98s became Oldsmobile's best sellers for the first time. **4.** In their final year, 60 series cars, like this 66 club coupe, were dubbed "Dynamic" instead of "Special." **5.** Two-tone paint schemes were a popular $12.50 option. **6.** A combination wood and metal Fisher body was now used on 60 series station wagons.

1

2

5

4

3

6

1. A base-model 1948 **Pontiac** had unadorned fender sides, as this Torpedo Eight two-door sedan demonstrates. **2.** The $2072 DeLuxe Torpedo Eight convertible was the priciest non-wagon Pontiac model. **3-4.** Streamliner coupes were available in standard trim starting at $1677. An additional $89 bought this DeLuxe version, which included front-fender trim, full wheel covers, and bright metal gravel guards. The Hydra-Matic automatic transmission became optional on Pontiacs for 1948. It proved very popular, as roughly three-quarters of '48s were so equipped. **5.** This ad pushed Pontiac durability and long-term reliability. **6.** This was Pontiac's last year for all-wood wagon bodies. Prices started at $2364.

1948	SCORECARD	
MAKE	**PRODUCTION**	**RANK**
BUICK	213,599 ▼	6th ▼
CADILLAC	52,706 ▼	15th ▲
CHEVROLET	696,449 ▲	1st ●
OLDSMOBILE	172,852 ▼	8th ▼
PONTIAC	235,419 ▲	5th ▲

1

2

1. Buick's Super and Roadmaster were completely restyled on shorter wheel-bases. The new Roadmaster Riviera, with its pillarless hardtop, became a style leader as soon as it hit showroom floors late in the model year. Early models had straight side trim, but later cars had the sweep-spear trim shown here. **2.** Starting in mid-July, the Riviera's sweep-spear trim was available on Roadmaster convertibles at extra cost. **3.** Riviera production was only 4343 units.

3

1-2. Buick's new station wagon body used far less wood than in previous years. **3.** "Ventiports," more commonly known as portholes, made their debut; Roadmasters had four, Supers and Specials had three. **4.** The second-most-popular Buick was the Super two-door sedanet. **5.** Specials soldiered on with the old B-body.

1

2

1. **Cadillac** ads paired cars with fine women's jewelry. **2.** Cadillac introduced a revolutionary new high-compression, overhead-valve 331-cid V-8 that put out 160 horsepower. The best seller in a record year was the Series 62 four-door sedan. **3.** Power windows and a power driver seat were standard on convertibles and optional on other models. **4.** Cadillac's 1949 grille was lower and wider than the previous version, now featuring one horizontal and five vertical bars. Convertible sales were up 47 percent to 8000 units.

3

4

1

2

3

1-2. A late-year release, the Cadillac Series 62 Coupe de Ville hardtop earned accolades for its styling. At $3497, the price of admission was high though; it cost only $26 less than the convertible. The hardtop was designed to combine convertible sportiness with coupe practicality. 3. The three chrome strips below the taillights of the 1948 Series 62s were gone in '49. Here, the $2966 Series 62 two-door fastback club coupe. 4. **Chevrolet** introduced all-new cars for 1949. Once again, Chevy bore a clear styling kinship to costlier GM cars, something buyers always seemed to appreciate. 5. In line with a 1949 industry trend, Chevy offered a true structural-wood wagon (shown) through midseason, then replaced it with a similar-looking all-steel version with wood-look side and rear body panels. Both were eight-passenger Styline DeLuxe models with an identical $2267 base price. 6. This Fleetline DeLuxe four-door sedan wears accessory headlamp shades, windshield visor, fender skirts, wheel trim rings, and whitewall tires.

4

5

6

1949

3

4

1. All **Oldsmobiles** adopted "Futuramic" styling for '49. The most-affordable model was the $1732 Series 76 club coupe. 2. The Holiday was Oldsmobile's new 98 hardtop. The price was $2973, same as the 98 convertible. 3. An 88 convertible, powered by Olds's new "Rocket" V-8, paced the 1949 Indianapolis 500. 4. The 98 DeLuxe club sedan was old news compared to the Holiday hardtop but still managed almost 12,000 sales. 5. The Oldsmobile 76 woodie wagon sold for $2895, almost $750 more than the next-closest 76 series car.

2

5

1

2

1. Pontiac's cars were redesigned for 1949, with flow-through-fender styling similar to that of the new-for-'48 Cadillacs. All models rode a 120-inch wheelbase. The Chieftain four-door sedan is shown. **2.** Streamliner four-door sedans started at $1740 with a six-cylinder engine and $1808 with the eight. **3.** A small amount of wood was still used in Pontiac wagons, but unlike previous designs, most of the '49's doors were steel. Later in the model year, steel panels covered with simulated wood replaced this last remaining cabinetwork. Streamliner DeLuxe wagons ranged in price from $2622 with the six to $2690 with the eight.

3

1949	SCORECARD	
MAKE	**PRODUCTION**	**RANK**
BUICK	324,276 ▲	4th ▲
CADILLAC	92,554 ▲	15th ●
CHEVROLET	1,010,013 ▲	2nd ▼
OLDSMOBILE	288,310 ▲	7th ▲
PONTIAC	304,819 ▲	5th ●

The Depression mercilessly thinned the ranks of American luxury automobiles, but it also crippled independent producers of medium-priced cars. Among the most severely wounded were Hupp Motor Car Company, founded in 1909 by engineer Robert C. Hupp; and Graham-Paige Motors, launched in 1927 by brothers Joseph, Ray, and Robert Graham.

For a time, these automakers were prosperous rivals, each offering six- and eight-cylinder cars known for fine quality and good performance. But when "hard times" set in, demand for Grahams and Hupmobiles began a sharp decline. Interestingly, each company pinned hopes for a sales turnaround on advanced styling. Thus, Hupp hired industrial-design whiz Raymond Loewy to create a radical 1934 "Aerodynamic" line. Graham countered with handsome "Blue Streak" models penned by the artful Amos Northup—plus optional supercharging. But nothing seemed to work, and both companies were all but broke by 1939.

In a last-ditch effort, Hupp and Graham teamed up on a remodeled version of the late 1936-37 Cord Westchester sedan, with rear-wheel drive instead of front-drive. The resulting Hupmobile Skylark and Graham Hollywood shared tooling acquired by Hupp general manager Norman deVaux, but used different engines. Alas, the complex Cord design was unsuitable for volume production (ultimately assigned to Graham), so just 319 Skylarks were built as 1940-41 models, plus a handful of 1939 prototypes. Graham managed a disappointing 1859 Hollywoods in 1940-41. With such poor results and a looming world war, both companies eventually fled the auto business for more-profitable pursuits that, ironically, provided the long-sought salvation. 1

Graham... FOR 1940

2

3

4

1-2. Graham aimed to be America's style leader with an undercut, slanted face that came to be known as the "shark-nose." This style was introduced in 1938, and made its final appearance for 1940. **3-4.** The 1941 Grahams—here a supercharged Hollywood six—were handsome cars, but the suicide doors and freestanding headlights looked dated by 1941. Graham stopped car production after a short run of '41s.

·1. The Hollywood/Skylark rear aspect was little changed from the Cord's.
2. Hupp planned a Skylark ragtop based Cord's convertible phaeton sedan, but only one prototype was built in 1939. The car was later updated to look like a '40 model, but it would be the only such Hupmobile built. **3-4.** Production of the Skylark Custom sedan totaled only 319 units before manufacturing ceased in July 1940.

GRAHAM & HUPMOBILE SCORECARD			
YEAR	MAKE	PRODUCTION	RANK
1940	GRAHAM	350* ▼	21st ▼
1940	HUPMOBILE	211 ▼	22nd ▼
1941	GRAHAM	1,500* ▲	19th ▲
1941	HUPMOBILE	103 ▼	21st ▲
*Figure estimated			

Hudson was founded in 1909 by eight Detroit businessmen and named for one of them, department-store magnate J. L. Hudson. Success came early. Through the 1920s, Hudson was usually among the industry's top-five sellers, thanks to its popular low-priced Essex line and smooth, handsome, medium-priced cars with six- and eight-cylinder engines. But the Depression devasted big-Hudson sales. Had it not been for a new budget line called Terraplane, launched for 1934, Hudson might have folded in 1940.

As it was, Hudson pushed on without Terraplane, offering redesigned but still conservative senior cars in a half-dozen series.

Offerings were pared and mildly updated for 1946-47, which was all the postwar seller's market required.

Then, a sensation: the innovative 1948 "Step-down." Named for its recessed floorpan, it boasted long, sleek "torpedo" styling, sturdy "Monobilt" unitized construction with protective perimeter frame rails, and a low center of gravity. It all made for one of America's most striking and roadable cars. Sales and profits revived, but not for long, as the Step-down was fast outclassed by Big Three rivals. With that and a money-losing move into compact cars, Hudson sought refuge in a 1954 merger with Nash, then vanished from the scene three years later.

1

#3,000,000

#1

1. Company president A. E. Barit sits behind the wheel of the three-millionth Hudson to roll off the assembly line, a 1947 Commodore Eight convertible. Next to it is the reputed first Hudson, a restored 1910 roadster.
2-4, 6. Hudsons got a new body and were fitted with independent front suspension for 1940. This $670 Hudson Six Traveler, as well as the step-up DeLuxe models, rode a 113-inch wheelbase and had a 92-horsepower 175-cubic-inch six. All 1940 Hudson coupes and convertibles could be ordered with a pull-out pickup box, the last year they would be offered. Other models rode wheelbases of 118 or 125 inches, with either a 98-102-hp 212-cid six or a 128-hp 254.5-cid eight. **5.** Hudson's brochure called the Six "The car to see with the 'Other Three'" (meaning Chevrolet, Ford, and Plymouth), and boasted of "America's lowest-priced Straight Eight."

1940	SCORECARD	
MAKE	PRODUCTION	RANK
HUDSON	87,915 ▲	11th ▼

1

2

3

1-2. Although they had just been restyled the year before, Hudson wheelbases were stretched three inches and rooflines lowered two inches for 1941. The Commodore Eight sedan rode a 121-inch wheelbase and cost $1035. The rear-hinged back doors opened "suicide" style. **3.** Hudson promoted its woodie wagons as both passenger and commercial cars; they seated up to eight, but the second and third seats could be removed for cargo. They were offered as the Super Six (shown) for $1297 and the Commodore Eight for $1383.

1

2

3

4

1. One of Hudson's big promotions for 1941 was "Symphonic Styling," which coordinated interior colors with exterior hues. **2-4.** Another Commodore Eight four-door sedan, this one in Majestic Maroon. Other body styles in the Commodore Eight line included a two-door sedan, three- and four-passenger coupes, a wagon, and a convertible, which gained a power-operated top this year. Prices ranged from $978 to $1254.

1941		SCORECARD
MAKE	**PRODUCTION**	**RANK**
HUDSON	91,769 ▲	11th ●

1

2

3

1, 3. Hudson's largest car was the Commodore Custom Eight sedan, which rode an exclusive 128-inch wheelbase; three- and four-passenger coupes were on the standard Commodore's 121-inch span. This model sold for a princely $1510 with a 254.5-cubic-inch eight rated at 128 horsepower. **2.** Although only General Motors had a true automatic transmission in 1942, Hudson introduced semi-automatic Drive-Master and also offered a manual transmission with "Vacumotive" automatic clutch.

1

2

4

3

1-3. Hudson offered convertibles in three trim levels, all on a 121-inch wheelbase. Commodores were the top dogs, offered in six- and eight-cylinder versions. This Commodore Six went for $1481, $52 less than the Eight. **4.** Due to war-materiel needs, chrome was restricted to bumpers on all cars built starting January 1, 1942; other trim was painted. In Hudson's case, these "blackout specials" were produced only until February 5, after which car production ceased until the end of the war.

1942	SCORECARD	
MAKE	**PRODUCTION**	**RANK**
HUDSON	40,661 ▼	9th ▲

1

2

1-3. Hudson returned after the war with cars that were virtual carryovers save for grilles with an indented center section. The entry-level Traveler and DeLuxe were dropped, leaving Supers and Commodores in six- and eight-cylinder form. As elsewhere, prices were up significantly; this Super Six convertible, which could be had for $1414 before the war, now demanded $1879. **4.** The first batch of postwar Hudsons is shown being loaded onto a train in September 1945.

3

4

1

2

3

1, 3. The two-tone paint worn by this Super Six four-door sedan was an extra-cost option on top of the car's $1555 base price. So were the whitewall tires and fog lamps. Unlike the prewar models, all postwar Hudsons rode a 121-inch wheelbase.
2. Hudson's most expensive closed car for 1946 was the $1774 Commodore Eight four-door sedan. As before the war, it came with a 128-horsepower 254.5-cubic-inch straight eight. Six-cylinder models kept their 102-hp 212-cubic-inch straight six. Dropped along with the Traveler and Deluxe models was the little 175-cid six.

1946	SCORECARD	
MAKE	**PRODUCTION**	**RANK**
HUDSON	91,039 ▲	9th ●

1-3. Only subtle detail changes marked the 1947 Hudsons: The hood medallion was new, the front bumper was altered, and a key lock was added to the driver's door. More noticed, perhaps, were the hefty price increases; this Super Six convertible now went for $2021, up $142. **4.** Hudson's new hood ornament was displayed prominently on the company's 1947 sales brochure, which stressed the car's safety and comfort.

1

2

3

4

1

1. A regal-looking Commodore Eight sedan could be yours for $1972. Still underhood was a 245.5-cubic-inch straight eight. 2-3. At the opposite end of the closed-car price scale was the Super Six coupe with a 212-cid six. In three-passenger form, it went for $1628; adding a back seat commanded another $116.

2

3

1947	SCORECARD	
MAKE	PRODUCTION	RANK
HUDSON	92,038 ▲	11th ▼

1

3

1-2. Hudson's radically redesigned "Step-down" '48s boasted a floor-pan that sat below the top of the frame, which helped give the cars their low, sleek look. **3.** Hudson had offered pickups before, but this one-of-a-kind prototype was the only one built in the Step-down design.

2

1

3

2

4

1. The Step-down design looked especially sleek as a convertible. A top-line Commodore ragtop brought $3057 in six-cylinder form, $3138 as an eight. 2. Dashboards adopted round gauges set toward the center. 3-4. A $2490 Commodore Eight club coupe is shown with stylish two-toning. 5. This '48 Hudson with dual controls served as a rather ritzy driver training car.

5

1948		SCORECARD
MAKE	**PRODUCTION**	**RANK**
HUDSON	117,200 ▲	10th ▲

1

2

3

4

1-2. The Commodore Six ragtop was an expensive beast at $2952, but that was more than $100 cheaper than in '48. With the Step-down design came a new six-cylinder engine that was bigger than the eight—262 cubic inches compared to 254.5—but not quite as powerful, yielding 121 horsepower vs. 128. **3-4.** The Super Six business coupe was the lowest-priced Hudson at $2053, but this one's original buyer made up for it by adding sideview mirrors, rear bumper guards, and a spotlight. All Step-down Hudsons rode a 124-inch wheelbase, three inches longer than in '47.

1

2

1. A '49 Super Six Brougham two-door could accommodate a family for $2156. **2.** Just $51 more bought a four-door version; this example wears optional two-toning. **3.** A single Commodore Eight was customized by coachbuilder Derham with a padded roof and interior partition, and you're looking at it. **4.** The representative first 1910 Hudson was rolled out once again to commemorate the company's 40th anniversary—and 3,250,000th vehicle.

3

4

1949		SCORECARD
MAKE	**PRODUCTION**	**RANK**
HUDSON	159,100 ▲	9th ▲

Henry J. Kaiser was the West Coast tycoon who contrived to build World War II Liberty ships with almost car-factory speed. Joseph W. Frazer was a successful auto-industry sales veteran. Each man wanted to build a car under his own name, and in July 1945 they joined forces to form Kaiser-Frazer Corporation. Kaiser, always thinking big, bought the huge B-24 bomber plant in Willow Run, Michigan, and ordered up a large, conventional six-cylinder sedan whose chief virtue was not being a rehashed prewar design.

Production began in June 1946 for two 1947 models, identical except for trim and pricing. The Kaiser aimed at the medium-price class, while the more-elaborate Frazer targeted the luxury field. Both versions were rather pricey, due to high postwar materials costs. But they sold well in a sell-anything market, and K-F came out of nowhere to run ninth in U.S. auto production for 1947-48. Journalists dubbed it "The Postwar Wonder Company."

After a standpat 1948, K-F gave its '49 models a moderate facelift and better-quality furnishings. Both makes added a convertible sedan, and the Kaiser line got a fixed-roof four-door "hard-top" version and novel "hatchback" utility sedans.

But 1949 was a big year for the Big Three, all of which had totally redesigned corporate fleets. Joe Frazer knew this in advance, and urged that production be trimmed until K-F could issue all-new products of its own. But Henry wouldn't have it, declaring "The Kaisers never retrench!" Instead, he tooled up for 200,000 cars and ended up selling just 58,000.

Leftovers were recycled as "1950" models. With that, a furious Joe Frazer resigned as company president; his namesake car was dropped after 1951.

K-F never recovered from this debacle. Even the beautiful new 1951 "Anatomic" Kaiser proved uncompetitive, and the company abandoned U.S. car production after 1955.

1

2

1. Henry J. Kaiser (right) and Joseph W. Frazer stand in camaraderie that wouldn't last into the 1950s. 2. Kaiser-Frazer took over the gigantic Willow Run factory, which had been used by Ford during the war to build B-24 bombers. At the time it was the nation's largest building under one roof. 3. Although neither of the cars were inexpensive, the **Kaiser** cost less: $2104 for the base Special (shown), $2456 for the top-line Custom. 4. Blessed with a bit more equipment and an upscale look, the **Frazer** Standard (shown) started at $2295, while the Manhattan went for $2712.

3

4

1

2

1-3. Of the two Kaiser and two Frazer models offered, by far the most popular was the cheapest: the $2104 **Kaiser** Special. This example is dressed up with whitewall tires, fog lamps, spotlights, and a sun visor. Interiors were subdued but boasted the widest seats in the industry. Although Kaisers were intended to make up the vast majority of sales, volume was nearly equally split. The two makes were very similar, both riding a 123.5-inch wheelbase and carrying a 100- to 112-horsepower 226.2-cubic-inch Continental six-cylinder engine. Kaisers and Frazers were sized and priced between contemporary Buicks and Cadillacs, both of which offered V-8 engines.

3

1-2. A Kaiser Special shows off its slab-sided body that may look plain today, but was sleek and almost futuristic in 1947. **3.** Although all production Kaisers and Frazers were four-door sedans, this one-off two-door Kaiser Special was built with a wrap-around rear seat and a front seat that could rotate 180 degrees to face rearward. **4.** A Continental six-cylinder engine sits on a skid at the Willow Run plant awaiting insertion into a 1948 Frazer.

1

2

4

1

2

3

4

1-4. Frazer's top-line car was the $2712 Manhattan. Frazer exterior styling was differentiated from that of the Kaiser with a unique full-width grille and "pleated" front and rear bumpers. Trim was also fancier inside and out. Manhattan's two-tone interiors featured seats upholstered in rich bedford or other broadcloth, or quality pleated leather. Combined Kaiser-Frazer production totaled nearly 140,000 units in both 1947 and 1948, amazing figures that put the company ahead of all other independents save for Studebaker.

1947-48		SCORECARD
MAKE	**PRODUCTION**	**RANK**
KAISER	1947 70,474	14th
	1948 91,851 ▲	14th ●
FRAZER	1947 68,775	15th
	1948 48,071 ▼	17th ▼

1

1. Kaisers received a mild facelift for 1949, gaining a wider grille, chrome lower side trim, and larger taillights. Also new was a utility sedan body style, which featured a hatch lid and lower tailgate in place of a conventional trunklid. It was offered in the base Special series as the $2088 Traveler (shown), which was $93 more than its conventional sedan sibling. **2.** Without actually saying so, Kaiser ads touted the Traveler as a station-wagon alternative. **3-4.** The utility sedan was also sold in the uplevel DeLuxe series as the Vagabond for $2288. All utility sedans had their spare tire mounted to the left-side rear door, which had an exterior handle but didn't open.

3

4

1. The $2195 Kaiser DeLuxe sedan was the most popular of the Kaiser-Frazer duo for 1949, but sales of all K-F models plummeted in the face of redesigned rivals from the Big Three. **2, 4.** Another new body style introduced for 1949 was the four-door convertible sedan. The center roof pillar was replaced by a glass pane that didn't roll down, though all the other windows did. As a Kaiser it was offered only in DeLuxe form for $3195, but only about 54 were sold. **3.** Taking the convertible sedan and adding a hard top resulted in the $2995 Virginian, which beat most Big Three hardtops to market by two model years. An estimated 946 were sold.

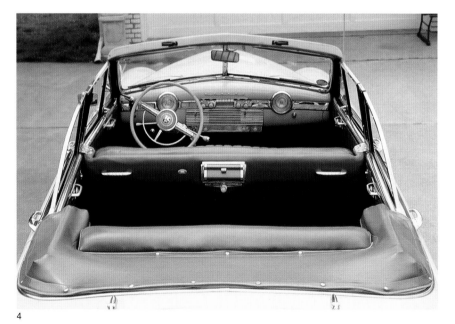

1

2

1-2. **Frazer's** '49 freshening brought vertical taillights and a Cadillac-like eggcrate grille. Shown are top-line Manhattans, which went for $2595 in sedan form. Two-toning was an option. **3.** Frazer's version of the convertible sedan was offered in Manhattan trim for $3295—$100 more than its Kaiser counterpart, yet it sold better: a whopping 70 vs. the Kaiser's 54. As a result, these cars are very scarce and valuable today. **4.** K-F buyers faced a completely restyled dashboard for 1949 that boasted huge, chrome-rimmed dials. Nevertheless, all the changes didn't much help K-F sales, and leftover '49s were sold as 1950 models.

4

3

1949		SCORECARD
MAKE	**PRODUCTION**	**RANK**
KAISER	79,947 ▼	16th ▼
FRAZER	21,223 ▼	18th ▼
All figures estimated		

Nash Motors took shape in 1916, when one-time General Motors president Charles W. Nash purchased the Thomas B. Jeffery Company of Kenosha, Wisconsin. The firm succeeded with medium-price cars in the Roaring Twenties, then struggled through the Threadbare Thirties. Indeed, Nash might have folded but for a 1937 merger with the Kelvinator appliance company. But that ushered in the visionary George Mason to guide Nash's future, which he did as well as anyone could have under the circumstances. Helped by handsomely redesigned 1939 models, Nash entered the Forties with sales restored to profitable levels.

The 1941 Nashes introduced a basic design that continued through 1948. Sturdy "single unit" construction was the headline attraction for a new six-cylinder economy series, the 600. The big Ambassadors still used body-on-frame construction though. These cars were far from exciting, but they did make money.

Nash did even better with its all-new 1949 Airflyte models. Not everyone liked the radical styling, but these unibody cars offered smooth comfort and huge interiors with exclusive "travel" features like reclining front seats. Alas, Nash floundered again in the Fifties, and only its popular Rambler compacts survived the make's belated departure after 1957.

1

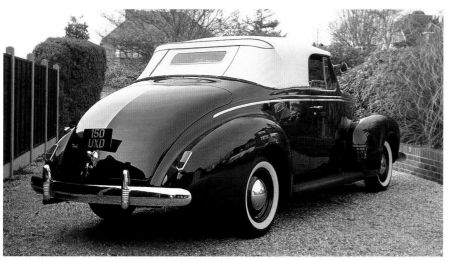

1. The last pre-war Nash, a 600 coupe in "black-out" trim, rolled off the line in early 1942. **2-3.** Nashes wore a minor facelift for 1940. At $1085 to start, the convertible coupe was the priciest and rarest Ambassador Six. Only 206 were built. **4.** Nash advertising touted comfort, quality, fuel economy, and exclusive features. **5.** The limited-production 1940 Ambassador Special Cabriolet was styled by noted California designer Count Alexis de Sakhnoffsky. Its custom touches included chrome trim removal, a cut-down windshield, and scooped-out door tops.

1

2

1-2. Overall demand for Ambassadors increased by 31 percent for 1940, but orders for the $985 Ambassador Six trunkback sedan nearly doubled, to 7248. 3. Nash's "Weather Eye" heating/ventilation system all but banished drafts and steamed-up windows by continually drawing outside air through the heater. 4. Prices started at $795 for a Lafayette business coupe. The Lafayette fastback four-door sedan pictured in this ad went for $875.

1940 SCORECARD		
MAKE	PRODUCTION	RANK
NASH	62,131 ▼	14th ▼

3

4

1941

1. Nash went to unibody construction for 1941, and became the first U.S. firm to produce an all-unitized, low-priced car. Curiously, only the entry-level 600 series had this innovation. Uplevel Ambassadors shared the unitized 600 bodies but also used a separate frame. Nash was likely hedging its bet in case unibody construction didn't catch on, but the 600 series was a success, and unitized body construction eventually became the industry standard. **2.** This two-tone 600 sedan and others in the series were promoted as gas-sippers, claiming 25 to 30 mpg; the "600" name suggested 600 miles on a 20-gallon tank of gas. **3.** The 600 rode a 112-inch wheelbase, while its Ambassador big brothers used a 121-inch span. The flagship of the new 600 line was the Deluxe trunkback sedan, which was introduced at a base price of $860. Coupes and sedans were introduced in October 1940, and a fastback two-door sedan in two levels of trim joined the line in December.

WITH A NEW KIND OF CAR_

Nash Enters the Lowest-Price Field !

★ 25 to 30 Miles per Gallon of Gasoline!
★ Flashing Pickup of New "Flying Scot" Engine!
★ Roomier than 1940 Cars Costing up to $200 More
★ A Coil Spring Ride on All Four Wheels!
★ New "Unitized" Steel Body~Safer, Quieter
★ Improved Weather Eye Conditioned Air System
   ...and Convertible Bed
★ Overall Economy Saves You $70 to $100 a Year!

Imagine-if You Can   THIS BIG 1941 NASH SEDAN SELLING FOR THE SAME DOLLARS YOU'D PAY FOR AN ORDINARY LOW-PRICE CAR!

Go **NASH** AND SAVE MONEY EVERY MILE

3 SERIES...17 BEAUTIFUL MODELS...ALL AT NEW LOWER PRICES!

1

2

3

1

2

3

4

6

5

7

1, 3. Ambassador Eights were powered by a 261-cubic-inch inline eight rated at 115 horsepower. Although this convertible's dual exhausts are nonstock, the right-side mirror and fog lamps are factory options. **2.** This ad proclaimed Weather Eye "the greatest health, comfort, and safety motoring feature of the last twenty years." **4-5.** Nash's six-passenger coupe was dubbed the Brougham. Items like the radio, bumper guards, whitewall tires, trim rings, and overdrive transmission on this Ambassador Six cost extra. **6-7.** Nash offered two kinds of four-door sedans: trunkbacks and "Slipstream" fastbacks like this $1020 Ambassador Six.

1941		SCORECARD
MAKE	**PRODUCTION**	**RANK**
NASH	84,007 ▲	12th ▲

1

2

1. This ad talked up Nash's economy, unibody construction, and coil-spring suspension, among other selling points. **2-3.** In addition to their shorter wheelbase, 600 models could be distinguished by their semi-skirted rear-wheel openings. The $993 trunkback sedan had the highest base price in the 600 line. **4.** A major facelift of all models resulted in distinctive styling, centered on a low, wraparound grille with a small auxiliary grille planted above. Some models sported fender trim that matched the horizontal bars in the grille.

3

4

1

3

4

2

1-2. Power for Ambassador Six models came from a smooth, 235-cubic-inch ohv L-head six that put out 105 horsepower. Pictured here are the $1044 four-door fastback and the $1009 Brougham coupe. **3-4.** All 1942 Nash dashboards dazzled with art-deco-inspired chrome and engine-turned metal trim. Broughams offered seating for six.

1942	SCORECARD	
MAKE	**PRODUCTION**	**RANK**
NASH	31,780 ▼	12th ●

1946

4

1

2

3

1. After World War II, eight-cylinder Ambassadors did not return. This Slipstream sedan shows off the revised grille, parking lights, and hood decorations ushered in for 1946. **2.** Only 272 wood-trimmed $1929 Ambassador Suburbans were built. **3.** The centrally located Weather Eye vent was a Nash-dash focal point. **4.** The '46 models were little changed, but that didn't stop Nash from bragging about cutting-edge "what's coming" features.

1946 SCORECARD		
MAKE	**PRODUCTION**	**RANK**
NASH	94,000* ▲	8th ▲
*Figure estimated		

1. For 1947, Nashes showed almost no appearance change from the prior year—the upper grille was a bit wider, but that was about the only difference. Frankly, there still wasn't much need of anything more drastic; this was the second year of the booming postwar sellers' market, and the main concern was simply to build as many cars as possible, since thousands of buyers were waiting. Company president George W. Mason began expanding the company. Nash purchased plants in El Segundo, California, and Toronto, Ontario, Canada, and, in anticipation of increased car production, began construction on a new 204-acre proving ground in Burlington, Wisconsin. **2.** The Ambassador had an elegant presence that belied its reasonable $1809 price tag. Nash production rose to about 101,000 units for the model year.

1

2

1

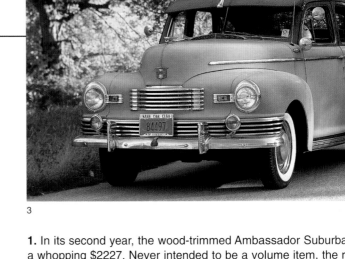

3

1. In its second year, the wood-trimmed Ambassador Suburban sedan sold for a whopping $2227. Never intended to be a volume item, the rustic Suburban tallied only 595 sales for the year. 2. The best-selling Ambassador was the trunkback sedan with 15,927 deliveries. 3-4. The 600's rear fenders retained the deeply skirted wheel arches that had been part of the car's look since its debut in 1941. The 600 was still being offered in only one trim level and, considering the two-door sedan did not return to the roster after World War II, in just three body styles. The $1420 four-door fastback continued as the most popular 600.

2

4

1

2

3

1-2. The lightest, cheapest, and least-popular '47 Nash 600 was the Brougham coupe. A total of 12,100 of the $1415 vehicles were built for the model year. **3.** An Ambassador sedan paced the 1947 Indianapolis 500 on May 30. **4.** Anxious postwar buyers were reminded that a new Nash was surely worth the wait.

1947	SCORECARD	
MAKE	PRODUCTION	RANK
NASH	101,000*▲	10th ▲
*Figure estimated		

1

3

2

4

1. "Cannon Ball" Baker piloted this 1948 Nash 600 to a new climbing record on New Hampshire's Mount Washington. **2.** Nash expanded its model line for '48, returning to a two-trim-level model roster. The Ambassador Super four-door trunkback sedan cost $1916. **3.** Last offered in 1941, the Ambassador convertible was revived this year. **4.** The $1858 Super Brougham was the lowest-priced Ambassador, listing for $189 less than its uplevel Custom sibling.

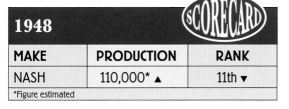

1-2. Orders for Ambassadors were on the rise in 1948. The most popular style was the fastback four-door sedan, with 18,920 built, but only 4143 of those came with the Custom trim seen on this example. **3.** At $2345, the Ambassador ragtop was the most-expensive Nash. It came exclusively in Custom trim. **4.** Nash advertising pulled no punches. This swaggering ad wanted to "bet" that all new cars would match the 600's innovative features by 1952. **5.** Dashboards were mildly revised but retained their round gauges and art-deco look.

1948	sCORECARD	
MAKE	**PRODUCTION**	**RANK**
NASH	110,000* ▲	11th ▼
*Figure estimated		

1

3

4

2

1-2. Independent automakers were forced to take enormous risks to remain competitive, and their gambles paid off surprisingly often, as with Nash's radical '49 Airflyte. The new car had unibody construction, functional streamlining (just 113 pounds of drag at 60 mph), and a one-piece curved windshield. As before, Ambassador models, such as this Super four-door sedan, used a 121-inch wheelbase. The 600s rode a 112-inch span. **3.** All models used a novel "Uniscope" gauge pod mounted on the steering column. **4.** Despite a narrow track, the Airflyte's turning radius was compromised by the "archless" front wheel openings.

1

2

210 x 78 x 62!

THAT'S NASH!

4

3

1. In addition to its main plant in Kenosha, Wisconsin, Nash also assembled Airflytes in El Segundo, California. 2. Weather Eye flow-through ventilation was carried over to the new models. 3. Partially assembled '49s make their way down the assembly line. 4. Bigger was better in 1949. "Nearly eighteen feet long, over 6½ feet wide—one sweep of racing curves from bullet nose to tear-drop back," this ad exclaimed.

1949	SCORECARD	
MAKE	PRODUCTION	RANK
NASH	130,000 ▲	10th ▲

Packard was born in 1899 and reached the summit of American luxury motoring by 1916. Its famous slogan, "Ask The Man Who Owns One," symbolized the patrician breeding, quality craftsmanship, and long-lived reliability that marked most every Packard through at least the 1940s.

Like its peers, Packard got through the Depression with medium-price six- and eight-cylinder cars, but enjoyed relatively greater success. As a result, a small, no-hurry automaker became a major industry power. In fact, Packard was often among the top-10 U.S. producers in the years just before World War II, not only outselling luxury rivals Cadillac and Lincoln but mass-market nameplates like Chrysler, Nash, and Hudson.

Packard redesigned its entire lineup for 1941. All models retained classically upright lines save the midseason Clipper sedan. Low, sleek, and beautifully formed, it looked like no Packard before. The public loved it—so much so that most every Packard was "Clipper-Styled" for war-shortened 1942.

This look returned for 1946-47. Packard was financially healthier than ever, thanks to lucrative wartime contracts. But management feared the Clipper would seem dated against new postwar Big Three designs. Accordingly, the car was reskinned for 1948, gaining "flow-through" fenders and a wider, lower grille. The result, alas, was dubious—some likened it to a "pregnant elephant"—and the modernizing added 200 unhelpful pounds. Still, sales held up in a booming economy. But the market soon changed, and that plus other factors led to a slow decline that ended in 1958, when the last Packards were built.

1

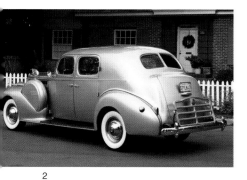

2

3

1. The medium-priced One Twenty was the car that buoyed Packard during the Depression, when high-end luxury cars were out of reach for most shoppers. Styling updates for 1941 did away with Packard's outdated freestanding headlamps. 2. A 1940 One Twenty club sedan cost $1239. 3-4. After the success of the One Twenty, Packard added the less-expensive, six-cylinder-powered One Ten. The $867 One Ten business coupe was the cheapest Packard of 1940. 5. The One Ten was by far the best-selling Packard line. With 62,300 built, it outsold the One Twenty more than two to one. This One Ten convertible coupe sold for $1104, $32 more than a Buick 40 Special.

4

5

2

1

1, 3. Designer Howard "Dutch" Darrin modified Packard convertibles in Hollywood. In 1940, Packard added Darrin models to its catalog. This car is one of two Super Eight sedans built by the factory incorporating Darrin features. **2.** Packard Darrins were a hit, but limited production couldn't meet demand. This Darrin-like sedan was built by coachbuilding firm Rollston.

3

1. Dutch Darrin lowered the hood and cowl of the standard Packard convertible and eliminated the running boards to create the Darrin convertible. Although fewer than 50 were built in '40, they added glamour to the Packard line. On the Super Eight One Eighty chassis, a Darrin convertible cost a hefty $4593. 2. The Super Eight One Sixty sedan was powered by a 160-hp straight eight. 3-4. Other Darrin signature modifications included a dip in the doors and a padded dash.

1940	SCORECARD	
MAKE	PRODUCTION	RANK
PACKARD	98,020 ▲	9th ▲

1

3

1-2. Packard integrated headlights with the front fenders for '41. Packard's digni-fied styling changed slowly so that a Packard was always recognizable and its gilt-edged resale value was protected. By the Forties, body styling was changing rapidly and Packards were looking old fashioned. This One Twenty club coupe is equipped with air conditioning—a Packard first in 1940. **3-4.** Packard offered woodie wagons in its regular line for '40 and '41. In common with most other makes at the time, Packard bought its wagon bodies from outside sources such as Hercules Body Co. of Evansville, Indiana. This One Twenty wagon cost $1541.

2

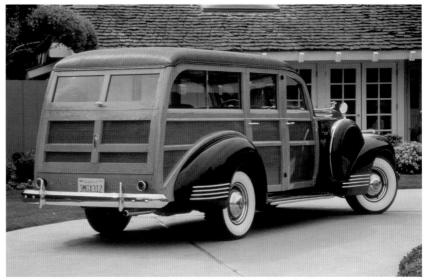

4

1

2

3

4

1-3. The One Twenty convertible coupe rode on a 127-inch wheelbase and weighed 3570 lbs. Its 282-cid straight-eight engine put out 120 hp. The One Twenty offered good performance, smooth operation, and high build quality. Packard's vertical-grille treatment for 1941 was flying in the face of the industry trend for horizontal front-end design. The '41-style bodies were short lived; new "Clipper" styling was introduced in mid-'41, and by '42 all series offered the new-style bodies. Only convertibles and limousines retained the upright '41-style bodies in '42. During WW II, the U.S. government approached Packard about selling its little-used '41-style body dies to the Soviet Union. Soviet Premier Joseph Stalin admired Packards and the postwar Russian ZIS car was his tribute to the luxury car of the American establishment. **4.** The One Ten two-door sedan rode a 122-inch wheelbase and weighed 3250 lbs. Its 245-cid six developed 100 hp. Thanks to its lighter weight, the One Ten's performance was almost as good as the One Twenty. Although these lower-priced models were diluting Packard's luxury image, their quality and durability never let the company down.

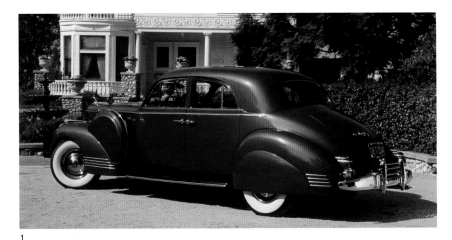

1

2

3

4

1. Although medium-priced cars dominated Packard sales, the senior-line cars were as luxurious and well crafted as ever. Packard commissioned LeBaron coachbuilders to supply 99 Sport Brougham bodies for the One Eighty chassis. **2.** This convertible sedan came off the line as a One Eighty formal sedan, and was converted to a ragtop in 1983. **3.** Packard's 356-cid, 160-hp Super Eight was more powerful than Cadillac's V-8. This Super Eight One Eighty formal sedan with overdrive could cruise effortlessly at 70 mph. **4.** This one-off One Twenty convertible with One Eighty trim was originally purchased by actress/ballerina Vera Zorina.

1941		SCORECARD
MAKE	PRODUCTION	RANK
PACKARD	72,855 ▼	14th ▼

1942

1. Packard introduced the Clipper midway through the 1941 model year, positioning it between the One Twenty and One Sixty. By '42 every Packard line offered a Clipper-bodied car, though designations such as One Sixty and One Eighty continued. Dutch Darrin designed the Clipper, and Packard's styling department made revisions. With Clipper styling, Packard went from old fashioned to cutting edge. Although the new cars were low, wide, and streamlined, they also had the dignity and elegance expected of a Packard. **2-3.** For '42, the One Twenty and One Ten lines were renamed Eight and Six, respectively. This Clipper Eight Custom sedan cost $1341. Power for the 282-cid eight rose to 125 hp. Six and Eight models rode on a 120-inch wheelbase, while One Sixty and One Eighty cars had a 127-inch span.

For 1942, *new Clipper styling* - in even the lowest-priced Packards!

1

2

3

1

2

3

4

1, 3, 4. Packard didn't have time to tool up a new Clipper convertible body for '42, so this Six made do with the old styling. **2.** General Douglas MacArthur ordered this Clipper Eight Custom sedan with virtually every option available—including air conditioning, overdrive, and radio. The $1341 base price nearly doubled to $2600. The factory returned the general's check and delivered the car to his station in Australia as a gift.

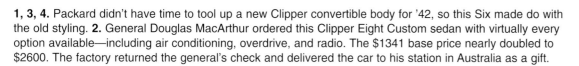

1942		SCORECARD
MAKE	**PRODUCTION**	**RANK**
PACKARD	33,776 ▼	11th ▲

Brand-new for '46—and, more than ever before, it's

AMERICA'S No.1 GLAMOUR CAR!

"We wish we had a thousand of them!" a Packard dealer wired us.

And we wish we could supply all the new 1946 Packard Clippers our dealers, and their customers, are clamoring for!

Thanks for your enthusiasm!

Right now, all we can say to the thousands of loyal Packard friends, is this: We are doing our level best to accelerate production, and we shall continue to apportion available

cars fairly among our dealers.

Naturally, we, too, are eager for you to become the proud owner of this magnificent new car—for it's

The Greatest Packard Ever Built!

In the brilliant flash of its performance . . . and in every sweeping contour of its speed-stream styling . . . it's for-and-away America's No. 1 Glamour Car!

And the new skills developed by Packard

master craftsmen in building high-precision combat engines for planes and PT boats, now bring you, in this great car, a mechanical excellence that is little short of perfection itself!

A Car Worth Waiting For!

So, if you have to wait a little while for your new 1946 Packard Clipper, we hope you'll be patient. Here is a car worth waiting for, if there ever was one!

★ ASK THE MAN WHO OWNS ONE ★

See the new

PACKARD
Clipper
FOR 1946

1

2

Styled and powered
for real economy

THE NEW PACKARD
Clipper Six

3

1. A GI returning from WW II is met by his wife in a Clipper Deluxe Eight sedan. **2.** The Packard line hums with low-price, six-cylinder, Series 2100 Clippers. Unfortunately, Packard shot itself in the foot when it diluted its luxury cachet with these models during a prosperous period when "economy" cars were no longer necessary for the company's survival. **3.** The Clipper was available as a two-door club sedan. This Clipper Six sold for $1680.

1946	sCORECARD	
MAKE	**PRODUCTION**	**RANK**
PACKARD	30,793 ▼	13th ▼

1

2

3

4

5

6

7

8

1-2. This $3140 Custom Clipper club sedan used the same body, engine, and chassis as the $2747 Super Clipper. **3.** Custom Clippers featured subtle luxury touches such as cloisonné emblems on the hubcaps. **4-5.** In the postwar seller's market, Packard could have sold every high-profit Custom Clipper it could build. Unfortunately, Packard chose to concentrate on medium-priced models with lower profit margins. The Custom Clipper sedan sold for $3449. **6.** Although not real wood as in most prewar Packards, the Custom's painted woodgrain interior trim was still elegant. **7-8.** As in previous years, Clipper Sixes found work as taxicabs, giving riders pleasing levels of room and comfort.

1947	SCORECARD	
MAKE	**PRODUCTION**	**RANK**
PACKARD	51,086 ▲	17th ▼

1

1-2. Packards had plump new styling for '48. Plush Custom Eight interiors were trimmed in wool broadcloth and leather, as seen on this $3750 four-door sedan. The Custom's 127-inch wheelbase was seven inches longer than other Packards—the stretch was required to fit its 160-horsepower, 356-cubic-inch straight eight. This exceptionally smooth engine used nine main bearings. **3-4.** Packard's first postwar ragtops debuted this year. The Custom Eight convertible cost $4295.

2

3

4

1

3

4

2

1-2. The wooden bodywork of the Station Sedan was structural only at the smallish tailgate. Wood at the door panels and window frames was inlaid. **3.** The Super Eight convertible was powered by a 327-cid, 145-hp straight eight. At $3250, it was almost $1000 cheaper than the Custom convertible. **4.** Packard's flagship was the $4868 Custom Eight limousine. The low-production limousine bodies were built by Henney Co., who also built professional cars on Packard chassis.

1948	sCORECARD	
MAKE	**PRODUCTION**	**RANK**
PACKARD	92,251 ▲	13th ▲

1-2. Packard celebrated its golden anniversary in 1949, but had little in the way of new styling to mark the occasion. Packard's "pregnant elephant" styling was initially well received, and 116,248 cars were sold for the 1949 model year. Sales slipped precipitously in 1950. The sturdy '49 Super Eight convertible weighed 4025 pounds. The Super Eight's 327-cid straight eight got a five-hp boost to 150 this year. **3-5.** The $2802 Super Eight club sedan was positioned midway between the luxury Custom and the entry-level Eight. **6-7.** The $2383 Eight Deluxe sedan arrived at midyear. It was powered by Packard's base engine: a 288-cid, 135-hp straight eight.

1

2

3

4

5

6

7

The world's largest maker of horse-drawn vehicles was 50 years old when it turned to horseless carriages in 1902. The South Bend, Indiana, company prospered anew through the Twenties with medium-priced Studebakers and a line of low-priced cars. It even contested the grand-luxe market by acquiring aristocratic Pierce-Arrow in 1928.

But Studebaker was hit hard by the Depression, and in 1933 was forced into receivership (akin to a Chapter 11 bankruptcy today). Fortunately, this crisis ushered in new managers who swiftly turned things around, selling Pierce, eliminating sales duds, and pushing full-bore on more-salable products. By 1936, Studebaker was out of the woods and back in the black. Then, the biggest success yet: the 1939 Champion, a low-priced addition to the year-old line designed by the redoubtable Raymond Loewy. It immediately became Studebaker's bread-and-butter. Another full redesign for 1941 gave South Bend a three-year sales winning streak that might have continued had World War II not intervened.

Studebaker resumed civilian production with a token crop of 1946 "Skyway" Champions, basically warmed-over '42s, then trumped establishment rivals by being "First By Far With a Postwar Car." Another effort by the Loewy team, the all-new 1947

Champions and top-line Commanders were low, sleek, and modern as tomorrow—exactly the kind of cars Americans were expecting. Though some couldn't tell if it was "coming or going," the '47 Studebaker was a major coup for an independent automaker, and the company enjoyed record sales and profits through 1950 despite few design changes.

Ultimately, though, Studebaker's haste proved misguided. As the Big Three realized, the war-starved early-postwar market didn't demand newly designed cars, just cars newly made. Had Studebaker waited until 1949, it might be with us today. Instead, the company was increasingly outmatched by larger competitors, and finally exited the car business in 1966.

1

4

3

5

6

1. The redesigned 1947 Studebaker Champion (left) looked far more modern than its '46 counterpart.
2-3. The economical Champion was first introduced in midseason 1939 and received only minor changes, such as sealed-beam headlights and a revised grille, for 1940. Edwards Iron Works of South Bend, Indiana, offered a slide-in box that could turn a Champion coupe into a coupe pickup. **4.** Midline Studebaker Commanders rode a 122-inch wheelbase and were powered by a 226-cid, 90-hp six. Note the contrasting color "Delux-Tone" paint treatment on this club sedan. **5.** Champion dashboards were reasonably classy for a low-price vehicle. **6.** The priciest Commander model was the $925 four-door Cruising Sedan.

1940	sCORECARD	
MAKE	**PRODUCTION**	**RANK**
STUDEBAKER	107,185 ▲	8th ●

Smart 1941 Studebaker

1

2

3

1. All 1941 Studebakers boasted new styling with slightly sharper noses and lower, wider, vertical-bar grilles. A Commander Land Cruiser sedan in topline Skyway trim is depicted in this ad, which urged shoppers to "Step up in distinction!" **2-3.** A President Land Cruiser sedan retailed for $1250 in flashy Delux-Tone trim. Note the unique "double-curve" rear fenders.

1-2. Presidents and Commanders came in a second four-door style: the six-window, suicide-door Cruising Sedan. This regal President Skyway version started at $1230. **3-4.** Thanks to its late-season arrival, production of the President sedan coupe was extremely limited, and restricted to Skyway trim. Only 477 were built. All Presidents used Studebaker's top engine: a 250-cubic-inch inline eight that made 117 horsepower.

1

2

3

4

1-2. Studebaker's 1941 sedan coupes are considered to be the first mass-produced vehicles with one-piece curved windshield glass. The Commander models shown here wear two-tone paint in their "color belts," a $5 option. **3-4.** Even humble Champions could be spiced up with two-tone pizazz. Cruising Sedan prices ranged from $795 to $860, depending on trim level. All Champions used a 169.6-cid, 80-hp flathead six.

1

2

3

4

1-3. The 1941 Champions wore an attractive scaled-down version of the Commander/President styling. As seen on this Club Sedan, cowl-mounted side air vents funneled fresh air into the interior. Champion dashboards lost their round gauges in favor of a de rigueur horizontal instrument panel. Note the pistol-grip parking brake handle beneath the dash. **4.** Each of the four Champion body styles came in DeLuxe, Custom DeLuxe, or Delux-Tone trim. Pictured in this ad is the $785 Custom DeLuxe Club Sedan.

1941	scORECARD	
MAKE	**PRODUCTION**	**RANK**
STUDEBAKER	133,900 ▲	9th ▼

1

2

3

4

5

6

1. All 1942 Studebakers wore a styling facelift with new full-width stainless grilles. This ad touts the new "Turbo-matic Drive" semiautomatic transmission, but wartime production needs intervened and only a handful of cars were so-equipped. **2-3.** A redesigned dash featured a circular speedometer in an engine-turned stainless steel instrument panel. A Commander Skyway Sedan Coupe commanded $1105. **4.** The $1045 Custom Cruising Sedan was the cheapest four-door in the Commander line. **5.** Spunky Champion models, like this $774 Custom Club Sedan, rode a 110-inch wheelbase. **6.** Studebaker renamed its midline trim level "Deluxstyle" this year. A President Deluxstyle Land Cruiser like this one could be had for $1241. President models retained their 124.5-inch wheelbase; Commander models rode a 119-inch span.

1942		SCORECARD
MAKE	**PRODUCTION**	**RANK**
STUDEBAKER	50,678 ▼	8th ▲

STUDEBAKER 173

1

3

4

1-2. Studebaker's 1946 line consisted only of the Skyway Champion series due to a nationwide steel shortage and the fact that Studebaker was readying itself for the midyear introduction of a strikingly restyled '47 line. The prewar Commander and President models were history. The '46 Champions were mildly updated '42s, with stainless-steel rocker trim and elevated parking lights among the few changes. Five-passenger coupes like this one went for $1044. **3-4.** The priciest and most-popular Studebaker this year was the $1097 Cruising Sedan, with sales of 10,525. All '46 Studes retained the prewar Champion's 80-hp six.

1946		sCORECARD
MAKE	**PRODUCTION**	**RANK**
STUDEBAKER	19,275 ▼	15th ▼

1947

1. Studebaker stunned the industry by bringing radically redesigned postwar models to market before any of the Big Three. New Champion and Commander models wore unorthodox styling by Raymond Loewy and Virgil Exner. The $1378 Champion DeLuxe three-passenger coupe boasted Studebaker's lowest 1947 base price. **2.** The Champion two-door sedan was available in topline Regal DeLuxe trim for $1520. **3-4.** Ads called Stude's new look "a melody in metal." Note the radical wraparound rear-window glass on these Champion (left) and Commander five-passenger Regal DeLuxe coupes.

1

A postwar thrill in style and handling ease...
the daringly different 1947 Studebaker

STUDEBAKER
First by far with a postwar car

2

New and wonderful in riding comfort, too
... the beautiful new 1947 Studebaker

STUDEBAKER
First by far with a postwar car

3

There's something about a new Studebaker
that gets people really excited

STUDEBAKER
The postwar leader in motor car style

4

1

1947 Studebaker Champion De Luxe Coupe for three passengers.

1947 Studebaker Champion Regal De Luxe Coupe for five passengers.

1947 Studebaker Champion Regal De Luxe 2-door Sedan for six passengers. This body style also available in the Commander model.

1947 Studebaker Champion De Luxe Convertible for five passengers.

2

1947 Studebaker Commander Regal De Luxe Coupe for five passengers.

1947 Studebaker Commander Regal De Luxe Convertible for five passengers.

1947 Studebaker Commander De Luxe Coupe for three passengers.

1947 Studebaker Commander Regal De Luxe 4-door Sedan for six passengers.

3

4

1, 3-4. Although they weren't available at the beginning of the model year, Studebaker did nonetheless field convertibles for '47—the company's first ragtops since the 1938-39 convertible sedans. The Regal-DeLuxe-only Champion droptop went for $1902. **2.** This colorful comparison illustrates the trim variations and six-inch wheelbase difference between Champion and Commander models.

1

2

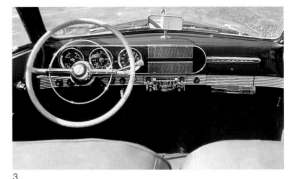

3

4

5

1-2. Studebaker changes for 1948 were mainly cosmetic: simplified bumper guards and more chrome across the top of the grille. The top-dog Champion model was again the convertible, which went for $2060 this year. **3-5.** At $2431, the Commander ragtop was the most-expensive '48 Stude. Commander dashes had a rounded gauge housing; it was rectangular on Champions. **6.** Production was up again this year, as most competitors were still selling warmed-over prewar designs. Studebaker continued to boast that it was "first by far with a postwar car." **7-8.** The $2265 Commander Land Cruiser rode an exclusive 123-inch wheelbase.

6

7

8

1948	SCORECARD	
MAKE	**PRODUCTION**	**RANK**
STUDEBAKER	184,993 ▲	7th ▲

1

1

2

4

1-3. For 1949, Studebakers again received only minor changes, including updated trim, wraparound bumpers, and a larger 18-gallon fuel tank. This Regal DeLuxe two-door sedan is accessorized with a sun visor, spotlights, and rear window blinds. Regal DeLuxes came with chrome ribbing at the bottom of the dash. **4.** Studebaker's unique five-passenger coupes were dubbed "Starlight coupes" this year. The Champion Regal DeLuxe version sold for $1757.

1

2

3

1, 3. The Commander line's six was enlarged to 245.6 cubic inches and bumped to 100 hp. The flagship Land Cruiser's longer wheelbase afforded a four-inch stretch in the rear doors, which made for outstanding rear-seat legroom. With a production run of 14,390 units, it was the top-selling Commander this year. **2.** This Stude ad pushed "new," showing a Commander Starlight coupe and the Land Cruiser's luxurious back seat.

1949	SCORECARD	
MAKE	**PRODUCTION**	**RANK**
STUDEBAKER	129,298 ▼	11th ▼

The biggest automotive drama of the 1940s starred Preston Tucker, a burly, ebullient industry veteran with experience in sales, engineering, and finance. During World War II he laid plans for a radical new car: a spacious Cadillac-size sedan with a rear-mounted horizontally opposed six-cylinder engine, all-independent suspension, and a strong girder-type chassis with "step-down" floor. Safety features abounded: protrusion-free dashboard; a windshield that popped out harmlessly on impact; and a front "Safety Chamber" for passenger refuge in a looming crash. Styling, by young free-thinker Alex Tremulis, was aerodynamically efficient and visually striking: a low-slung torpedo-shaped fastback with prominent fenders, doors cut into the roof, and a central "cyclop's eye" third headlamp that swiveled with the front wheels.

With all this, plus brisk performance and secure handling—confirmed in 1948 by *Mechanix Illustrated*'s Tom McCahill—the Tucker seemed too good to be true. Yet Preston was serious, showing a drivable prototype, lining up dealers, and landing a bargain-priced war-surplus bomber factory in Chicago. But he had a knack for making enemies, and evidence suggests that his venture worried, if not threatened, the Detroit establishment—and its Congressional delegation. Worse, he moved with suspicious haste in floating a $15 million stock issue to start production. That led to charges of "fast sell" tactics, a probe by the Securities and Exchange Commission, and an avalanche of damaging publicity.

In the end, Tucker Corporation built

just 50 cars, all in August 1948, plus the prototype "Tin Goose." In October 1949, Preston and seven associates stood trial on 31 counts of conspiracy and securities and mail fraud. All were acquitted in January 1950, but by that time there was no hope of salvaging Tucker's grand dream. Sadly, Tucker died a broken man in 1956 at the age of only 53.

1

2

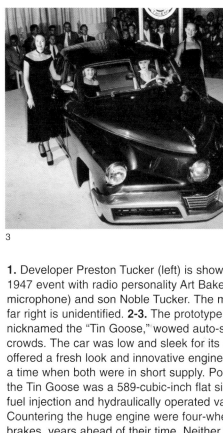

3

1. Developer Preston Tucker (left) is shown at a 1947 event with radio personality Art Baker (with microphone) and son Noble Tucker. The man to the far right is unidentified. **2-3.** The prototype Tucker, nicknamed the "Tin Goose," wowed auto-show crowds. The car was low and sleek for its day, and offered a fresh look and innovative engineering at a time when both were in short supply. Powering the Tin Goose was a 589-cubic-inch flat six with fuel injection and hydraulically operated valves. Countering the huge engine were four-wheel disc brakes, years ahead of their time. Neither the engine nor brakes made it to production versions, but both remain on the Tin Goose, which survives to this day in a private collection.

1

2

3

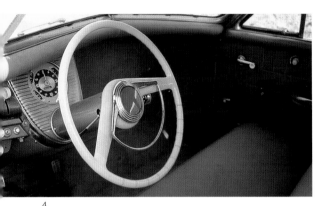

4

5

6

1-3. Tucker's Torpedo combined futuristic lines with industry-leading performance and numerous safety features. It was powered by a rear-mounted, 335-cubic-inch, 166-horsepower flat-six helicopter engine that exhausted through six tailpipes below the rear bumper, and underneath lay an advanced fully independent suspension. A center headlight turned in the direction the front wheels were steered. 4-5. In place of a conventional dashboard, the Tucker had a padded crash rail, beneath which was a "Safety Chamber." Instruments were contained in a steering-column-mounted pod. 6-7. Just 51 Tuckers, including the prototype Tin Goose, were built, and most of these novel cars survive today.

7

Willys built passenger cars long before it built Jeeps. It all started in 1907, when car dealer John North Willys bought ailing Overland and set up in Toledo, Ohio. Renamed Willys-Overland, the company was number two in the U.S. industry by 1918.

The Twenties saw Willys offering a broad line of four-, six-, and eight-cylinder cars. These included low-cost Whippets and comfortable medium-priced Willys-Knights with the smooth, quiet sleeve-valve engine design developed by Charles Yale Knight. But several setbacks had left Willys relatively small and weak, so it suffered more than most automakers in the Depression. After declaring bankruptcy in 1932, the company reorganized around just one model, the new four-cylinder Willys 77 compact. This evolved with various yearly improvements, but sales were never sufficient for a solid recovery, so Willys was still financially vulnerable as the 1940s opened.

Help had arrived in the person of supersalesman Joseph W. Frazer. At his behest, the 1939 Overland, a much-revised 77, was restyled for 1940, then updated again as the patriotically named 1941 Americar. The latter was arguably the best Willys in years, yet sales were disappointing.

What finally revived Willys was the wartime Army jeep, which it built by the boatload along with Ford and to a lesser extent American Bantam. Somehow, Willys managed to claim the jeep as its own creation, even though it wasn't. But most GIs called it a Willys jeep, and their huge affection for it suggested a huge peacetime market. So instead of postwar cars, Willys shrewdly devised the civilian Jeep CJ and two spinoffs: an all-steel station wagon and the jaunty Jeepster convertible. These and continued military production should have been enough. Instead, Willys made an ill-fated return to passenger cars for 1952. As a result, the Willys name gradually disappeared, though it lingered on in South America through 1967.

1

2

3

1. Willys were facelifted for 1940 with a new nose that included flush-mount headlights and a split horizontal grille. All models were designated "440," which stood for "four cylinders, 1940." 2. Willys' first station wagon, the $830 DeLuxe wagon, was the most expensive model in the lineup. 3. Willys coupes and sedans came in baseline Speedway or uplevel DeLuxe trim, which netted extra chrome hood trim, dual wipers, and bumper guards. A DeLuxe sedan cost $672. 4-6. A minor freshening for 1941 included a one-piece grille. A DeLuxe coupe cost $685, up $44 from 1940.

5

4

6

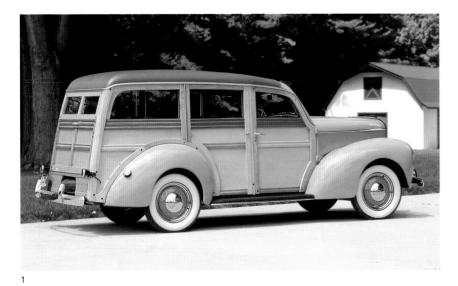

1-2. The Willys lineup was expanded for '41, and all cars assumed the patriotic "Americar" monicker. An upscale "Plainsman" trim level for coupes and sedans was added above the Speedway and DeLuxe series. Prices ranged from $634 for a Speedway coupe to $916 for the DeLuxe-only wood-bodied wagon. Willys' 134.2-cubic-inch L-head four gained two horsepower, to 63, this year. **3.** Despite this year's two-inch wheelbase stretch to 104 inches, Willys remained squarely in the compact economy car category. By comparison, 1941 Chevy cars rode a 116-inch wheelbase. This factory photo illustrates the Willys' relatively diminutive overall dimensions. **4.** Simple, sleek Willys dashboards featured a symmetrical design with a centrally located horizontal speedometer.

1

2

3

4

1. Willys' ½-ton pickup shared the car's front end styling. 2. The 1942 Americars were little changed, save for various detail improvements and a vertical chrome strip that bisected the grille. 3. Though Willys didn't invent the jeep, they did perfect the design, provide the powerplant, and build the majority of jeeps used in World War II. Willys-produced jeeps were labeled MB models and were manufactured in Toledo, Ohio. The four-cylinder "Go-Devil" engine was good for 60 horsepower.

1

3

1

2

3

4

5

6

1-2. After the war, Willys abandoned traditional passenger cars in favor of jeep-based vehicles, hoping to capitalize on the good reputation the military jeep had earned in battle. The Jeep Station Wagon arrived in July 1946. It boasted a jeep-style front end design and a 104-inch wheelbase from the prewar American car. The all-steel body was something of an industry first; a few low-volume commercial station wagons had appeared earlier with steel bodies, but never in any volume (except for the Chevrolet Suburban), and they were totally truck-based. Willys marketed the Jeep Station Wagon as a car. The Willys wagon anticipated a whole new class of vehicles that we now refer to as sport-utilities. **3.** The panel delivery was an easy spin-off of the wagon. **4-5.** Early Jeep wagons—here a '48—were painted maroon and given a simple wood-look paint job, which designer Brooks Stevens specified because he felt people expected a wagon to look like a woodie. **6.** Instrumentation was contained in a central pod.

1

2

1. Willys aimed for a more-carlike vibe with the Jeepster, a jaunty phaeton convertible introduced in July 1948. The hood, fenders, grille, and 104-inch-wheelbase chassis were borrowed from the Jeep Station Wagon. Jeepster production reached 10,326 during the model's debut year. 2. The Jeep CJ-2A was a civilian-spec MB. Differences included larger 7-inch-diameter headlights and a drop-down tailgate. 3-4. The Jeepster's $1765 price included such niceties as overdrive, bumper guards, white-wall tires, wheel trim rings, and a steering wheel with a full horn ring.

3

4

1

3

1. For 1949, Willys dropped the Jeepster's base price to $1495 to better compete with its Big-Three rivals. The majority of '49 Jeepsters were four-cylinder models, but a new $1530 VJ3-6 version—with a 148.5-cubic-inch six—was added during the year. The changes were little help—sales plummeted to a mere 2960 for the model year. **2.** The hardy CJ-2A Jeeps retained the stark functionality of their military kin. **3.** The 1949 Willys Station Wagon was little changed from previous models. This is a two-wheel-drive model, but 1949 saw the addition of optional four-wheel drive.

WILLYS		SCORECARD
MAKE	**PRODUCTION**	**RANK**
1940	21,418 ▲	17th ●
1941	7,517 ▼	17th ●
1942	6,833 ▼	16th ▲
All figures estimated